# K. SCHILDER

*Professor of Systematic Theology at the Theologische Hogeschool of De Gereformeerde Kerken in Nederland, Kampen, The Netherlands. from 1934 to 1952.*

# Christ and Culture

Translated by
G. van Rongen and W. Helder

**PREMIER**
WINNIPEG
1977

Schilder, Klaas, 1890-1952.
Christ and Culture

Translation of Christus en Cultuur.
ISBN 0-88756-008-3

1. Christianity and Culture. I. Title.
BR115.C8S313     261.5     C77-002118-2

**PREMIER PRINTING LTD.**
1249 PLESSIS ROAD, WINNIPEG, MANITOBA, CANADA R2C 3L9

# Preface

Almost twenty-five years ago, on March 23, 1952, the LORD took unto Himself His servant Klaas Schilder. The present translation of one of his works thus appears at a very appropriate time.

*Christ and Culture* is the English translation of Schilder's *Christus en Cultuur*. The original version of this publication was issued in 1932 under the title "Jezus Christus en het cultuurleven"; it was included in *Jezus Christus en het menschenleven*, a collection of contributions by various authors. In 1947 it was published separately as *Christus en Cultuur*; a reprint followed in 1953.

The author was born on December 19,1890, in Kampen, The Netherlands. In his native city he later studied at the Theologische School of De Gereformeerde Kerken in Nederland, from which he graduated *cum laude* in 1914. After having served as minister in several congregations, he was in 1933 awarded the doctoral degree *summa cum laude* at the Friedrich-Alexander University, Erlangen, Germany. His dissertation was entitled *Zur Begriffsgeschichte des "Paradoxon," mit besonderen Berücksichtigung Calvins und des Nach-Kierkegaardschen "Paradoxon."* In the same year he was appointed Professor of Systematic Theology at the Kampen Seminary, which post he held until his death in 1952.

Dr. K. Schilder wrote numerous books and articles. His trilogy *Christus in Zijn lijden* became internationally known especially in its English version, *Christ on Trial* (1938). He regularly contributed to the weekly *De Reformatie* ever since it began publication in 1920, becoming one of its editors in 1924; from 1935 on, he was its only editor. The strong stand that he took, not only in theological and ecclesiastical matters but also over against the anti-christian philosophy of National-Socialism, led to his arrest by the Nazis in August, 1940. Soon after his release he was forced to go into hiding, for he was among those wanted by the German occupying forces. He remained in hiding almost until the end of the Second World War.

Twice, in 1939 and in 1947, Schilder visited the United States of America. The return voyage in 1947 provided him with the opportunity to revise and expand his above-mentioned 1932 essay. The preface to the new edition of *Christus en Cultuur* was signed and dated: "On board s.s. Veendam, August 24, 1947." This Dutch publication attracted attention also in the English-speaking world, particularly in the U.S.A.; for example, Schilder's ideas, together with those of Aurelius Augustine, John Calvin, and Abraham Kuyper, were thoroughly discussed by Henry R. Van Til in his *The Calvinistic Concept of Culture* (1959; repr. 1972). A Japanese translation by Professor Y. Yamanaka of Kansaigakuin University, Takarazuka, Japan, was published in 1974.

The present English translation was made possible by the kind permission of Mrs. A.J. Schilder-Walter and the cooperation of the original publisher, T. Wever, Franeker, The Netherlands.

May the LORD bless this publication and use it in the battle for true culture.

Grand Rapids, Michigan, U.S. A.                    G. van Rongen
Hamilton, Ontario, Canada                          W. Helder

December, 1976

# Christ and Culture

1. "Christ and culture" — this theme has occupied the minds of many as long as Christianity has had a place in this world. Rather, it did so already many centuries before. For the name "Christ" is nothing but a translation of the word "Messiah." Even during the days of the Old Testament, when the Messiah was still expected, men thought, struggled, and prophesied about as well as rebelled against the "Messiah" (Christ) and "culture." If what we are about to write is true, then this age-old theme will continue to strain the attention in joy as well as in sorrow until the end of time. The complete solution also of this problem will not be reached in the course of time but is reserved for the day that will put an end to time. It will not be obtained in the way of evolution but along that of the catastrophic parousia of Christ Himself. Therefore the great joy and the deep sorrow about the final outcome of the struggle concerning Christ and culture can be expected at the end of the ages. Here one utters two heavily charged words: heaven — and hell.

2. The above already makes it clear that the theme which we are broaching here must not be inserted in the list of subjects that the hasty heathen takes into his sphere of interest *before* and the careful Christian only *after* the academic discussion thereof. The problem of the relation between Christ and culture immediately concerns the fundamental questions of Christian thought and action. Therefore a Christian must continuously contend with it. The one who does not touch it neglects his direct calling. The definition of a Christian's life-task as it is given in Lord's Day 12 of the Heidelberg Catechism and in which a Christian is considered as a prophet, a priest, and a king, is so ample and comprehensive that the matter of the relation between Christ (and the Christian) on the one hand, and cultural life on the other, is under discussion as soon as the question is raised how the pertinent words in this section of the Catechism must be interpreted. For this reason in particular, a confessing Christian is not allowed, before entering into the cultural struggle, to wait quietly (*ad calendas graecas*) for academic resolutions regarding the cultural problem. Neither has he permission to wait for what is more and more becoming their substitute, the resolutions or conclusions of a conference.

For life builds up the academy, but the academy does not build up life. At best it can think about life. The same way the problem of

the right appreciation of culture or that of the evaluation of a concrete situation which a Christian comes across or has to help create in
a given cultural phase, must never be reduced to a so-called merely
academic matter. Life precedes the academy: *primum vivere, deinde
philosophari.* Everyone has to deal with a temporally and locally
determined phase of cultural life. At his birth he is thrown into the
midst of it, and no one is able to withdraw from it, not even for one
single day, supposing that he would be allowed to do so. Man cannot
isolate himself, though he may flee into a cloister that does not distil
liqueur or anything like that, nor helps to fill the pages of a magazine.

3. Why is this problem such a difficult one? Many things could be
said in explanation. We shall mention a few points only.

a. One of the main reasons is that the opinions so widely diverge.
Not only in what we sometimes too abstractly call the world, but also
in what — again we must say, often in too abstract a way — is called
the church, we see the struggle between opinions that are very much
each other's opposites. There is nothing unusual in this. Those who
really adhere to the authentic philosophy of pure materialism will
have a view of culture that completely differs from that of people
who think along the lines of metaphysical universalism. Those who
think that history is linear set up a construction that is completely different from that of the man who sees history as a cycle. The theist
and the pantheist are one another's opponents, also in their con-
ception and appreciation of culture. A Lutheran's evaluation — if
only he is loyal to Martin Luther — will differ from that of a Calvinist;
that of a pessimist is not the same as that of an optimist. A Platonist
differs from an Aristotelian, a Spinozist from a Cartesian, a Kantian
from a pupil of Fichte. Even among the Romantics Goethe does not
agree with Novalis, nor Schleiermacher with the Schlegel brothers.
We did not even mention Bismarck and Rosenberg, Otto and Walt
Whitman, or the Buddhist of one sect or another. The differences
which divide the philosophers will influence the theologians and the
ordinary church members. It is only a dream if someone believes that
"the cultural idea" is a sort of master-key opening the door to the
conference hall that offers a peaceful reception to cultural
congresses. It will be war there — that is to say, if the participants in
the conference have their wits about them, which unfortunately is
unusual.

b. A second factor, then, is that time and again the problem itself
is given new solutions which — even within the same period — contradict each other. Or that it takes the shape of theoretical foun-
dations. All this happens in as well as outside the church. Both

concepts, "Christianity" as well as "culture," are thus frequently created, fixed, and used in different senses. Consequently the problem of "Christianity and culture" is in the (as we shall see later on: incorrect) opinion of many people — wittingly or unwittingly — narrowed down to a problem of "*religion* and culture," or of "nature" and "grace," which are then repeatedly considered as two separate territories. Indeed, the word "territory" is easy to handle. However, it is mostly used in a too strongly geographical, not to say, mathematical sense. And mathematical concepts (such as e.g. a point, a line, a plane, a "territory") do not find their correlative equivalents in reality. Besides, one may perceive that even then many questions appear one after another.

*c.* To all this must be added that the devaluation of the name Christ caused also the devaluation of the concept of culture. The church started to trifle with the name Christ, and philosophy did the same. As a result they also trifle with the problem of Christ and culture. As soon as two concepts are devaluated, the right track that must be followed by those who search for the relation between them is blotted out.

*d.* One has only to consider how those who call themselves church, broken adrift from the contents of the Confession of Faith, speak about the Christ. What is Christianity? Who is *Jesus* Christ? What is the historical position of this Jesus in the world and His significance for historical life? Does He have any influence at all on our historical life with its continuous relations? Is He indeed the incarnate Word of God, or is He (rather: he) no more than one of the many *Gestalten* of God's Word? Is the *Gestalt* of the Word of God an adequate revelation of its *Gehalt*, or is the *Gestalt* the paradoxical opposite of the *Gehalt?* Is the historical Jesus of Nazareth the fulfilment of the Old Testament expectation of the Christ (the Messiah), or is the messianic idea not adequately revealed in Him, or perhaps only fragmentarily? What does the *name* Christ mean? What does God intend with the name Messiah? What does His anointing mean? Does it really include a divine *commission* ("His being ordained"), and also a real *gift* ("His being made capable"), or are these two only designated in a symbolic way? Is there a fundamental difference between those "anointed ones" whom we consider as ordinary men and Jesus of Nazareth as One anointed in a completely distinct way? Or is this suggested fundamental difference no more than a fiction only? To what extent can He, as a historical person, act in human life in a critical, that is, judging and absolutely decisive manner? Does He Himself, as Jesus, as a historical person, together with our whole human life, lie under a crisis, that is, under a radical judgment of God

9

that condemns the world as this, as *our* world, or did He let us hear on earth, in a pure and effective, lively, judging and sifting way, the voice of God as the perfect Judge and perhaps also as our Father, the voice of the supreme and, in fact, unique criticism, repelling or attracting? It is actually something to weep about, but it is a matter of fact that in the circles of what is called Christianity there is much serious dispute about all these questions nowadays. And so we stand there as a concrete or legendary "community" of "Christians"; we all lay claim to this name, and get angry as soon as the one denies it to the other. But in the meantime we are very uncertain about the *fundamental questions* concerning Jesus and concerning Christ, at least among ourselves. Neither are we sure about each other. Opposing each other we stand with a series of written and especially unwritten Christologies in the midst of a multifarious world which claims that it is continuing to build up its "culture." And although we repeat a thousand times in tense and agitated Christian protest that the culture of this world is not mature and not pure, that it is deceptive, and that the reward of (also cultural) sin is death, the question is urgent and hurts so deeply, especially *as question*, whether we ourselves are not (at least as a group) completely unauthorized and unable to utter even one single word on this problem, because of our profound differences with regard to the term "Christ" as we find it in the problem of "Christ and cultural life." We are more and more active as a group in international, interdenominational, and interconfessional, ecumenical relations, and in sending out all sorts of messages concerning world life and culture. But it all lacks power, for as a group we no longer know *Christ*. As long as Jesus Christ, for us as a group, is not the Known One and the Familiar One, we utter nothing but immature statements about the relation between Christ and cultural life. For the first of these two terms is already hazy. And an international, inter-academic, ecumenical haze is the worst of all.

*e.* Is the situation any better as far as the second term of our problem is concerned, namely, cultural life? What actually is culture? The answers differ. We have already referred to that in a few words. However, it is really oppressing that in spite of this we still present all sorts of nervous, hurriedly fabricated and even, as far as our own point of view is concerned, illegitimate constructions. The worst part is not that the culture-philosophers time and again supply widely divergent answers to the fundamental issues. The worst part is this, that while all sorts of culture-philosophers entrench themselves behind a certain — as a matter of course, subjectivistic — theory *of value*, Christians, even confessional ones, fail to ask themselves more and more if not the first and actually only true value is that of the covenant communion with God, that of the assurance of faith, the value of Christian gratitude, which in a practical syllogism assures faith from the fruits thereof that it is *true* faith. The worst part is the servility with which Christian confessors, as soon as they touch the problem of culture, timidly look up to the unbelieving culture-philosophers next-door: Would they be so kind as to grant us a nod of approval? The progressive submission of Christian thinkers and theologians to (non-Christian) cultural and other philosophers, is more and more becoming an obstacle to giving a unanimous and unequivocal answer of faith. The youth leaders of today and lecturers of adult education classes, as far as they have a Christian background, realize perfectly well that the drafting of a concept of culture meets multiple and searching questions. At their conferences they toil with the problem of history, that of the individual and society, of the essence of the nations and the distinct races of men, of time and eternity, of physics and metaphysics, religion, morals and natural law, of evolution and creation. But about the fact that we as Christians have to take our startingpoint in *the prejudices of faith*, and that we have to accept upon authority, and consequently to act accordingly, that our positive and negative attitudes must merely and solely be a matter of faith, which (as we confess in our Catechism) is a sure knowledge and a firm confidence — about all this one can hear quite often as long as certain points of systematic theology (ecclesiastical suspensions included) are at stake, but one hardly hears the same things as soon as the sphinx of cultural life comes under discussion. There is much pride in the many words that are spoken on the theme of right action, but in the meantime the speakers do not discern the oppressive fact that this whole ideogram of "culture" and "cultural life" remains very hazy, and that one can work with it only on a premature and hypothetical basis. It is an artificial term that many people operate with; however, they do so without being justified philosophically, theologically, and, above all, as far as the concrete service of the living God is concerned.

*f.* When finally we act as if we really have established a connection between "Christ" and "culture," then the main question is not always put to the fore: What is it actually all about? Are we talking about culture as such (*the* culture) or only about *a* certain kind of culture? Is there indeed *a* permanent *culture*, which may be known by the peculiar style to which it is faithful, or do we, if we keenly discern things, find only a chaos of cultural *tendencies*? If it is not culture as such but only a particular form of culture, which is it then? *The* national culture or just *a* national one? *The* or *an* international culture? *The* or *a* temporary one? *The* or *a* future one? Is it a (or

11

the) culture which we have created or have to create, let alone are able to establish — that is to say, we as Christians? Or is it a sort of ideal culture that we are required to acknowledge or to hope for? Do we as Christians have to act in this world and its culture in the way of reform and revolt? Are we capable of doing this? Or have we perhaps been given only the limited task that we might somehow or other force our way through the rapid currents of this world's multifarious life, and thank God afterwards because the ship of our life just missed being wrecked in the tremendous energy of the breakers? Is there really a positive task for us as Christians? Does "following after Jesus" then really include the tireless actualizing of a God-given creative ability unto a peculiar (or distinct) Christian culture with world-conquering tendencies? Can the "following of God" be recognized in certain concrete acts in conformance to the material contents of divine commandments, and also in an accordingly concrete and steady attitude? Or is the following of God a formal concept only: God did indeed create the world, but He also permanently changes it, and once will do so in a catastrophic manner, wherefore only those can follow Him who replace any "yes" spoken to the existing world by "no" and thus consider any attitude as being of the devil, the revolutionary as much as the conservative attitude, and vice versa? Is a Christian's action performed in earnest or just as a game — by virtue of a fixed ordination that does not permit us anything but the game, and thus makes the game into the only possible "earnest"?

4. Innumerable are the questions that have not been answered, and, indeed, that have not even been formulated yet. "Jesus Christ" and "cultural life" have alternately been called enemies and friends, or even complete strangers one to another. The one, with Tolstoy, sacrifices "culture" to (his) "Christianity"; the other, with Nietzsche, abandons Christianity in favour of "culture"; a third one flares up in anger as soon as he hears that Christ and culture are considered to be connected with one another (cf. the contemporary, Barthian-inspired, criticism of a so-called neo-Calvinism). The startingpoint of the first two views — partly also of the third one — is an antithetical relation between Jesus Christ and cultural life, real as well as potential. On the other hand there are also those who, eagerly or with the feeling that they, too, are fortunately still allowed to participate, raise the slogan that Jesus Christ and "culture" can certainly be reconciled with one another and that the relation between the two may ultimately be considered an amicable one.

It may be unintentional, but the inevitable result of all this is, of course, that among those who swing back and forth in this manner practice reveals many greatly varying aspects. According to the one there is no higher task for a Christian than timidly to eat under the table "the crumbs which fall from the table" of unbelieving "culture builders," and consequently he defends this timorous eating with the thesis that in cultural affairs God has not imposed teetotalism. He, then, will never get beyond a questionable *argumentum e silentio*: What he *wants* has not expressly been forbidden; it is therefore all right. Do not ask him whether this eating of crumbs from the table of others is a meal of faith and love or a gesture of embarrassment, with a corresponding argument of embarrassment providing the necessary rescue. The other, however, jauntily asserts himself in cultural life, puffs up his little Christian person to a certain cultural pride, and keeps himself convinced that it is nothing but an argument of embarrassment when the above-mentioned brother, sighing and apologizing a thousand times for his meals of crumbs, quotes the apostle Paul and says, that one "cannot go out of the world" (I Corinthians 5:10). He in fact brands this argument as inferior. In his opinion it must be replaced by the proud watchword that a Christian has to promote God's honour "in all spheres of life," cultural life included. However, the crucial question, what "cultural life" actually is, and, in close relation with it, what exactly the sphere or territory of cultural life is, most likely remains unanswered for the time being, even by him.

We are fog-bound. Even the followers of Dr. Abraham Kuyper are. For years and years they talked of nothing but "God's honour in all spheres of life." The more scholarly ones among them constantly repeated Kuyper's adage concerning "sphere sovereignty." Every "sphere" of "life" had its own "sovereign." However, often they do no more than repeat this slogan. No wonder. For Abraham Kuyper himself could not clearly explain what exactly those "sovereigns" in all those "spheres" are. One single Sovereign — that we can accept and understand. But as soon as one starts to speak about "sovereigns" in the plural, each of them in his own sphere, then things become vague. When Kuyper says that God created everything "after its kind," he only repeats a biblical datum. However, it is really a big leap from "law of nature" to "sovereign." It is also a big leap from a creature of *God* to a product of *man*. And the same must be said about a third one, the leap which he makes from the respective *kinds* of creatures to the so-called "spheres" in which they play their role either with or without the help or hindrance of man. Kuyper's metaphorical language is here also a *metabasis eis allo genos*, a matter of mixing up unequal and heterogeneous quantities.

This is disastrous, in particular when one speaks about "spheres," each having its own sovereign. Really, we are fog-bound.

5. Now the sky can clear up only if we quietly put ourselves under the preaching of the Scriptures. They are fundamentally nothing but a revelation from God, knowable and known in Jesus Christ, His Son. Therefore no one can derive from their teachings anything concerning the theme of "*Christianity* and cultural life" unless he lets them reduce the problem to the matter (not of "*Jesus* and cultural life," but particularly) of "*Jesus Christ* and cultural life." It is no doubt very useful to consider briefly why the first two formulations of our theme are never able to penetrate to the foundation of our problem, while only the last-mentioned one really can. As soon as we have found the answer to this question, we believe that we are holding the clue to our subject as the Scriptures present it to us.

6. Actually, as we said, the problem should not be formulated as "*Christianity* and cultural life." For this formulation would not bring us to the root of the problem. As a matter of fact, by "Christianity" one can understand among other things: (1) the *community* of Christians (in the proper sense of the word or not, including or not including those who are Christians in name only), and (2) the *visible result* which it was possible to record in the visible world because of the Christian activities of the community of Christians, or, rather, which was, and time and again still is, recorded within the framework of a more or less fixed *communis opinio*. Of course, the word has many more meanings. However, let us leave them for what they are for convenience' sake. For even when we restrict ourselves to the just-mentioned two meanings of the word, we have enough problems. As for the first definition, what, for example, does "community" mean? Is it just the simple fact of being together, or the possibility of gathering together for those who call themselves Christians, correctly or incorrectly (*sun-ousia*)? Or is it a spiritual unity, spiritual in the sense of produced by the Spirit of God? In other words, is it a unity that is in conformity with God's Word (*koinōnia*)? Is this *koinōnia* the result of the efforts of man, something that *must* come into existence by his actions, or is it the product of God's efforts, something that *has* come into existence and now calls on people to act accordingly by acknowledging the communion which God has made, *de jure* as well as *de facto*? Or, as far as the second definition is concerned, is one, for the registration of such a *result* of Christian communion, dependent on history and tradition, or can every age thrust upon us its own theory concerning

this registration and qualification? "Christianity" is a difficult word — if one wants to go into the matter.

Nevertheless, in whatever sense one may take this word, one thing is certain: it is impossible to take "Christianity" as one's startingpoint when one wants to ask questions regarding cultural life, let alone solve the problem of "Christianity" and culture.

a. This is impossible in the first place because Christianity can never be the standard. Take (in the first of the two above-mentioned meanings) Christians together as a *community*, and then — if you could, by theoretical abstraction (for you cannot get any further!) — purge this community of all those who are Christians in name only. Or (according to the second meaning of the word) take Christianity in the sense of the *result* of the Christian (in your ideas even supposedly catholic) creed in man's and the world's life, and even be as strict here as you can in applying the standard and in bestowing the title-of-honour "Christian." Whichever way you would take it, in neither of the two cases would you be able to derive from this "Christianity" a *standard* for dealing with your problem. No Christian can be the standard, neither can a factual datum be. Facts do force our hands: no one can dispose of them, and everyone's actions rest upon the facts. Our hands can easily beat the air, but this does not result in or lead to anything. Only when they are put into the material produced by reality as it has historically developed, they are able to fashion this material. And as for this fashioning of the material (our acting with responsibility), we fully depend on the standards which God has established. The latter do not force our hands, they command us. Only the Word of God, Holy Scripture, is the standard; not the Christian or Christianity, but the speaking *Christ* Who has been made known to us by revelation, and Who also Himself "explains" God to us, and as the Giver, Keeper, and Interpreter of the Law speaks God's Word to us without any restraint caused by sin or impotence, He Who has been sent to the people on behalf of God. Any historical trend, also any cultural trend or construction, that would be based on Christianity as a datum or even on an ideal Christianity, which is a product of the mind, must necessarily end in sin, violation of the Law, and irreligion; it would be able to establish nothing but a Tower of Babel. For by taking a wrong startingpoint it has already started to do so. This way also historical materialism and positivism have taken the courage to orate on Christianity and culture. This way (though proceeding from different presuppositions) idealism, too, in more than one form, has done the same thing. This way even Barthianism has sometimes done so, when it said, "*Es predigt*": there is the *fact* of "preaching" in Church, which fact is then the startingpoint

15

for further theoretical development. There is a certain quantity called "Christianity." However, this *fact* is not the foundation of any *doctrine*, although every doctrine must take into account all facts, also this one. Facts do not form a foundation for doctrine. On the contrary, there is already a certain measure of doctrine in any description of a fact (or of what is considered as such). When there is a thunderstorm, this is a fact. But those who believe in Wodan and those who can explain it and have become acquainted with the theory of electrical discharges understand and describe this fact in completely different ways.

There is even more than this. "Christianity," as it takes shape in the midst of the world, carries the name of its own choice, and can be registered, is itself always deeply involved in a current cultural process or even in a series of cultural processes. Followers of Hegel, and consequently also Marxists, and National-Socialists, count Christianity itself among the cultural phenomena: the suppliers of the theories that were chartered by Anton Mussert[1] wanted to entrust the "Department of Culture"[2] with the interests of Christianity (which could be protected only in the European part of the Kingdom of The Netherlands). This already shows how seriously and inevitably "Christianity" itself — even if it were only to protect its name — is always involved in the clashing of the cultural trends that are present in every constellation of world life. Besides, it varies according to local, national, anthropological, and even climatological types. In brief, the term "Christianity," taken in this sense, is a sphinx, and nothing else.

*b.* And to the extent that it is no sphinx but can be allocated in history in a pure or (which is something different again) fixed shape, it has on its part often interfered in the cultural struggle in a high-handed and arbitrary way and with many shortcomings and sins. In every subsequent process of formation, deformation, or reformation, it sometimes tried to become a real and direct cultural force (remember the papacy), or lived, either consciously or unconsciously, from certain principles which put on its work-programme a clear *cultural* commission as its essential task. Of course this was wrong. For Christianity is not a matter of culture. Although, on the other hand, culture is certainly something that Christianity is concerned with. But according to the ever-repeated (although not biologically or evolutionistically determined) action of deformation and reformation, historical Christianity has never been able in the course of the ages to lead one specific cultural idea to victory, neither has it ever fully completed any of its mandates regarding cultural life. One will find here the most extreme variations: there is a vast distance between cultural imperialism — as it was developed by the Church of Rome in certain periods — and the isolated position, separatism, and asceticism of the "pious" but culture-shy people and congregations that are of the opinion that they represent true Christianity only in this sort of shyness. Who would be able to derive a cultural *standard* from such a "Christianity?" Neither is a majority or a minority decisive in this respect. Justice as well as power, health as well as healing gifts, they can belong to the majority, but also to the minority, even to the smallest minority one could imagine.

7. In the second place: History confirms that, strictly speaking, the problem cannot be formulated as "*Jesus* and cultural life" either.

For, to put it strongly, if no more is added to it, "Jesus" is of no use as far as our problem is concerned. We have to consider that Jesus has explained Himself as the Christ. This Self-explanation (according and with reference to *the Scriptures*) is accepted upon authority by the one and rejected by the other. This rejection is often camouflaged under the cloak of ignorance. The complaint is: He is such a *riddle*; please allow *me* to pray the prayer of the ignorant, in order to learn how to qualify this Jesus! Presently one will himself construct some Jesus-image or other. Not God's Sent One, Jesus Himself, but a human concept of "Jesus" is also *made* into a sphinx by those who do not acknowledge Him as *the Christ*.

However, He is not a sphinx, for His Self-explanation is clear enough. But He becomes one to those who dispose of His Self-explanation. Then for these people a riddle is propounded in Him, and this riddle is not disclosed as long as Jesus is acknowledged only as "Jesus." And old maxim used to say: *Ubi vides, non est fides*; that is, wherever something can be seen, no faith is needed. We will not analyze this adage; it can be well meant, but in general terms it is not correct. People could see the "historical Jesus"; but, in order to really know and acknowledge Him, faith was needed. The fact that the man Jesus was God's Christ (Messiah), that He was called the "son" of Joseph, though without having been begotten by him, and much more than this, remained a matter of faith. *Ubi vides, ibi fides. Visio quaerit fidem. Fides quaerit intellectum.*

This thought in fact preceded Christianity. For the Bible has never restricted itself to a speaking of "Jesus" only. In the Old Testament it first spoke of "Christ" (Messiah). But the fact that this *promised Christ* would later appear under the name of "Jesus" was then not yet known. However, since He did come, the Bible always speaks, as a matter of fact, about *Jesus Christ*. Before "Jesus" as a historical person came into this world, He was announced as *Christ*.

That is to say, God described His office and work in its quintessence *before* His historical appearance under a human name, in a human shape, and in a particular cultural situation, was even vaguely defined. Remember only the protevangel in paradise. When after many centuries during which God, by means of the prophets, had spoken about the coming Christ (Messiah) and given information in advance about His office and work, this Messiah came into the world and was registered as the son of Joseph and Mary and was called "Jesus," then everyone had to learn to consider this "Jesus" as the fully authorized *Christ*, unless Jesus was to remain a riddle to him with a supposed appeal to his own pretended authority to interpret. A *supposed* appeal, we said, for the real Jesus is terribly angry with those who refuse to accept the key to the interpretation of His person and work from the hands of God's anointed Prophet and Teacher. He then comes to such a generation — usually it is a majority — with visitation, or with punishment. Both fall upon His unwilling hearers-interpreters as often as He in the gospels, first of all to His first "contemporaries" but to us, too (who are also the contemporaries of the living Christ, Who governs us from heaven), speaks in "parables." Also concerning the subject of serving God in cultural life He repeatedly speaks in parables to His "contemporaries"[3] of the days of old as well as (via the Bible) of these days, and He reveals the meaning of these parables, also in cultural-theological respect, to those only who afterwards interrogate Him about all this (today via His Word) in faith. Of what benefit would "Jesus" be to us if nothing else were to follow, if no second[4] name, no second office-name, the name *"Christ,"* were added to this first one? The gospels do not give a biography of Jesus. Neither do they design their own image of Him. They already tell us that in our thinking we are not to go beyond that which is written (concerning Christ, in the Old Testament) (I Corinthians 4:6). They do not intend to give a *scientific*-systematic summary of His life's work from any formal and methodological point of view, not even from any cultural point of view. Any systematic treatise on Jesus' works, teachings, prophesying, building up and breaking down, is lacking in the Scriptures. The Gospel is neither a biography nor a novel. Neither does it describe a cultural phenomenon according to cultural-philosophic or cultural-historical methods, nor does it write Church history after the method of the science of historiography. The Gospel is not even a systematic exposition of the history of *salvation*. Therefore every effort that wants to learn only from a so-called *Life of Jesus* what He meant and still means in a particular aspect of human life is doomed to fail. For we have no *Life of Jesus*. Whoever consciously would like to write it, would strain himself in the telling and do injustice to Him. One can and may never separate the gospels — which describe to us the course that Jesus Christ followed towards and through human life in fulfilling God's counsel and in accordance with God's revealed will to remain Himself in evangelic redemption — from Old Testament prophecy; nor from the history of salvation and revelation, out of which He came to the fore according to plan — just as this history itself is of Him and determined by Him; nor from the epistles of Paul and the other authors of the New Testament epistles; nor even from the Apocalypse, with which the Bible completes its cycle. This Apocalypse, too, contains a description of history, not only concerning the future, but also concerning the past (Revelation 12, e.g.), and even concerning what was contemporary to John, its author (e.g., regarding Rome's emperor-worship as anti-christian moment, chapters 13 and 18). Also this last Bible-book lets us hear the revealed truth regarding the background and constituent elements and trends of any kind of history, cultural history included; e.g., that there is a *satanic* urge behind the anti-christian beast (Revelation 12), and that any struggle, the cultural one included, is fundamentally the struggle between the seed of the woman and the seed of the serpent; it is the *old* serpent that in any *new* cultural period persecutes the *old* "church-as-woman" and her one "Seed" and intends to annihilate them.

To summarize it all, no one is able to characterize the work of "Jesus" in a faithful way, as long as it has not become clear to' him from the whole of the Scriptures what Jesus came to accomplish as the Christ and what He therefore, as God's office-bearer par excellence, has to do in and for and also with the cosmos. The biblical preaching of "Christ" must in its contents absolutely determine already in what manner one is to speak about the biblical stories concerning "Jesus."

8. Actually this is not so strange. No one has ever been great in this world without having to be explained and understood partly on the basis of the time in which he lived, but also partly with reference to his own personality, that which the Father of spirits endowed him with individually and exclusively. However, as far as "Jesus" is concerned it is actually still different. As we have already said, in His works He is never understood in isolation from, but, definitely, also not on the basis of the time which He spent here on earth among men. He is known also by means of, but not on the basis of, His days. For He dominates, directs, and governs all ages. For Him the "fulness" of time does not mean a casual "occasion" or, as something

19

quite fortuitous, the fertile soil into which He, "finding" the field, could sow whatever He wanted, but it was His time, the "*kairos*" — *taken* by Him, as created for His sake — in the "*chronos*" extending according to God's plan. Neither can He be explained on the basis of the cultural history of "the nations" nor on the basis of Israel's history of salvation, for of both these "histories" (which are fundamentally one and of one territory) He is the foundation, the Worker, and the "Firstling," the beginning, the principle, the aim, and also the new startingpoint. The study of Hellenism cannot explain Him, even though it will be essential for the distinctive interpretation of His words and works (and vice versa). Neither does the knowledge of Judaism "explain" Him, although — provided that it produces good results — it sharpens every interpreter's pencil. The "faithful Witness" Who speaks continuously, but Who only as far as unbelief is concerned sometimes speaks in riddles, is Himself not a sphinx. O no, He never is. But a "Jesus *concept*," formed in innumerable variations by people who do not know Him as the Christ, and an *image* of "Jesus" arbitrarily designed — this is what time and again vexes its designers and worshippers with the quiet and mocking smile of a sphinx. The latter is again and again placed near the great caravan-routes of mankind. However, who decides which is the most important and the central one of these routes if the Bible is not permitted to decide? This sphinx can be seen standing in the midst of time. But who will put an end to the discussions — which are being revived also in this century — about the real nature of "*die Mitte der Zeit*"? This sphinx, which since the beginning of this era no eye has seen nor ear heard but the contours of which time and again loom up in the hearts of many people, is passed by many centuries. But it is silent, completely silent — unless "Christ" has been found in "Jesus" throughout the Scriptures. For Jesus Christ used to speak and He is still speaking: He is "present" with His Godhead, majesty, grace, and Spirit, speaking in His Word. Until the moment that one listens to Him, one can only compose fiction about this sphinx but not prophesy concerning it. Jesus must be put in His *own* light. Rather, He has to present Himself to us in His own light. But in this presenting and explaining Himself in His own light, Jesus is already doing the work of *Christ*. It is precisely in this work that He is the Christ, God's Prophet, Priest, and King. The light which does indeed shine in Jesus, shines in Him because He is the Christ, the Servant of the LORD. He does not allow us to isolate "Jesus" from "Christ" — not even in the academy, since it is not permitted "in life."

Is there still any reason to be astonished because people are so strongly divided with regard to the question what the importance of

"Jesus" is for cultural life, and because the problem "Jesus and culture" is given almost as many "solutions" as there are minds brooding on this problem?

No, it cannot be otherwise. And in the inevitability of this oppressive phenomenon His greatness is revealed and His judgment executed. For therein we find a proof in the negative of the horrible seriousness which is evident in the sanctions of His positive commandment that we are never to "see" Him as "Jesus" but always fully to "hear" Him as "Jesus Christ." For otherwise these "sanctions" come into force. The history of the "Jesus paragraphs" in cultural-historical works is so confusing that they make us think of a cultural-historical judgment: "Because they seeing see not; and hearing they hear not, neither do they understand" (Matthew 13:13). Any arbitrariness in constructing a "Jesus image" receives its own reward: it has to share the field with a multiplicity of the most individualistic views. We have already pointed out some of the bad harvests produced by this noxious soil. However, remember that it is of "Jesus" that one wants to speak: then the harvest becomes even more audacious and depressing. The Marxist places "Jesus" in cultural history as the great revolutionary. Ernst Haeckel utters his oracles on Jesus as despiser of culture. Constantine the Great saw in Him the most successful propagandist of a most Christian cultural struggle. Oswald Spengler places Him — Jesus! — among the historical pseudomorphoses of Arabic culture. Chamberlain sees in Him the founder of a moral culture. Hegel connected to "Jesus" a sort of cultural pantheism — this was done by him who apart from this was yet so wise as to remember that no one can isolate himself here from the trinitarian motifs of the early Christian way of representing things. Many people, for whom the sun rose only at Stockholm or Lambeth, where they wanted to formulate the "third confession" — where is it now? — saw in "Jesus" the great formulator of direct "messages" to the cultural world on the so-called topical cultural questions, although it must be said that the direct character of their "messages" can be obtained only at the cost of a fundamental vagueness. Again other convention delegates present themselves as inspired apostles or as inspiring mahatmas and they, too, render "Jesus" a small place among the "wise" who have left behind a sufficient number of enigmatic sayings to provide a lasting connection between "East" and "West." That way the traditional "Teacher" of the West is transformed in this encounter into an equally traditional "Patriarch" from the East. The Western world always had its "Teachers" *speak*, while the East prefers to hear (!) its "patriarchs" *keep silent*. The former express their conceptual learning in their many lines of writing, while the latter between their few lines make us guess at their strictly paradoxical thoughts, deriding any conceptual "clarity," which is then regarded as but a lack of clarity. This way "Jesus" as yet becomes a cultural factor, not so much because of what the theologians have heard Him say, but because of the fact that the theosophists heard Him keep silent: the "sphinx" is here no accident but the only suitable figure. And hardly have these people been together in conference, leaving behind a "message" also concerning Jesus, or, look: ascetics, mystics, sectarians of another kind, consider "Jesus" as entirely indifferent to culture. He only speaks of God, they say, and to "the soul," and in "the heart," but for the rough and tough life of the big world He does not, in their opinion, want to utter a single word apart from that of permanent separation: Go out from Babylon, separate yourselves! Theologians belonging to the school of modern *Religionsgeschichte* put "Jesus" in one line with Mohammed, Zarathustra, and other "founders of religion" and do not wish to hear of a factual distinction between true and false (pseudo-)religion; at best they will consider a distinction between degrees of divinatory capacity. And several chiliastic sects, which all through the centuries have nibbled not only at scholastic-hierarchical but also at living, reformationally sound Christianity, consider "Jesus," strictly speaking, as the grim prophet of their own cultural egotism and separatism: abruptly they dare to establish a private community that, in a life withdrawn from the suction of the world, is looking for the borderline which once will separate the world and the Church for ever.

9. Also the "church" itself is at fault here. Even she often neglected to see in "Jesus" and in all He did and did not do the "Christ" of God. She is guilty in so far as she allowed theologians to lift the four gospels out of the whole of the list of Bible-books and to abandon the totality of biblical teachings if only they could distil from the gospel data an "objective" "Jesus"-image. As long as one restricts one's attention to "Jesus," one may at best perhaps be able to say what "Jesus" has *not* done with respect to the cultural question; however, one will not arrive at a *positive* answer. For in order to be able to give a positive answer we must, apart from the name "Jesus" (His first name-of-office), take into account the (second) name "Christ." Those who only reckon with the "Jesus" of historiography, neglecting the prophecy that comes to us in the name "Christ," do not get any further than small wares: an exemplary interpretation of text-fragments, a parallel, a comparison, a parable. Such mere pedlary sometimes awakens feelings of pity when with the help of

some small details of the gospel story it distils certain contributions to a doctrine concerning "Jesus as cultural theoretician." The gold, incense, and myrrh of the Nativity story then sometimes have to serve as proof that He does like riches and wealth. We are often referred to the fact that He let Himself be served by the money of some rich persons, e.g. the wife of Chusas, king Herod's steward, as a detail intended to teach us that Christ instructs "the Church" to make a *rule*, if possible, of what was once for Israel an *emergency* measure and a retaliatory measure sanctioned by special decree: spoiling "the Egyptians." The costly ointment with which He let Himself be anointed in the presence of Simon, His host for the moment, His entering into the house of rich Scribes to eat with them, even the garment that was gambled away by soldiers at the foot of Calvary's cross and which was "without seam, woven from the top throughout," they all serve as illustrations in object-lessons about such problems as "Jesus and good taste," "Jesus and riches," "Jesus and culture." We shall refrain from mentioning more.

But does one not perceive how insignificant all this is? The gold and myrrh and incense are not mentioned again in the Gospels. The money was perhaps spent on a flight, the flight to Egypt. The Rabbi from Nazareth did not add to the money that He accepted but it was spent on the ministry of the Preacher of the Gospel of God's Kingdom. The costly ointment was accepted, not in order to teach the disciples anything about wealth and the use of wealth, but in order that Simon would submit himself to a preaching that put him to shame, or to teach His disciples — it was high time — concerning His imminent death. In the latter case this ointment was then presently added to the supply of funeral ingredients.

What can one do with this sort of "data" if one does not know more than this? Is this then a *cultural* image: "The foxes have holes, and the birds of the air have nests; but the Son of man hath not where to lay His head" (Matthew 8:20)? Is this really a cultural-technical datum: "When they chase you away from one village, go to the other and shake off the dust of your feet (Matthew 10:14)?

And if one does not want to hear any questions but only assertions, well, here they are. He withdrew partners from a flourishing fishing business, James and John. He made, no, not some masked culture types but unmasked fishermen, even from Galilee, follow Him, the Nazarene. One of them speaks his own dialect when he timidly slips into the court-room where the great court-case of the world is decided. He heals lepers, although sporadically; however, He does not establish leper-houses. He opens the eyes of the blind — again, sporadically — but He leaves others in their blindness; at any rate, He does not establish an organization for the support of the blind. For such a miracle He once uses mud. Although He is offered a royal crown, He does not accept it. He makes His entry intò the capital while sitting on the young of an ass. He deals carefully with servants, and when one of His disciples injures the ear of a certain slave called Malchus, He heals the man; but it is in vain that one looks for the beginning of an Association for the Abolition of Slavery. He looks those who have been possessed by demons deep into the eyes and leads them to the light; however, He never built a clinic, and did not make any preparations for that — at least, not in any direct sense. And the authors called by Him later on issue books, gospels, that show a complete lack of any artistic style and that are written in the common language of the people. Again we ask: Does one make any progress by trying to define and solve the problem with the help of this sort of details? Can one in this way even contribute to its solution?

10. Perhaps someone is of the opinion that we are not completely fair, and certainly not serious, in presenting the above collection of curiosities from this petty retail trade. Instead of these details, would he prefer to see the life of Jesus in broad outline?

Well, this can be arranged.

But the result will be the same, even then.

We shall mention a few points only.

When the Rabbi of Nazareth was here on earth, Judaism — just to mention one thing — was of almost no significance at all as far as the plastic arts were concerned. The background of this frequently observed phenomenon could not have been entirely praiseworthy in His opinion. For more than once it is evident that He was a seer and a prophet. The seer knows what is in man, and the prophet time and again brings it into relation with the rules given in the Scriptures. Therefore His keen eye and His prophetic insight made it clear to Him — more than it would be possible with us — that this deficiency was — at any rate, was also — the result of a wrong interpretation of the second commandment which the Father of Jesus Christ had given in the Law of the Ten Commandments to His people Israel and to all the nations. We would be utterly wrong if we were to apply Christ's complaint and accusation that the Jewish leaders had made God's commandment null and void by their human ordinances only to those few ethical maxims concerning which the average reader of a Church magazine asks the editor of the question column for clarification: Are we allowed to eat blood-sausage, to ride our bikes on Sunday, to marry our cousin, and things like that. The unproductiveness which, with respect to the plastic arts, distinguished the Jews from almost all the civilized nations of those days and later, *must*, in as far as a wrong interpretation of the second commandment was involved, have seemed a gap to the true and Spirit-filled Law-interpreter and as such must have hurt Him. One can express this opinion without prejudging the question whether the plastic arts are included by Christ among the concrete assignments which he gives to His soldiers on their pilgrimage of the "last days." For suppose that He with respect to the plastic arts does not unconditionally wish to give His people a mandate; still He can never take under His protection a sort of negativistic and ascetic ethics as far as it originates in a wrong interpretation of the Law of God and intends to be a God-pleasing document of this wrong interpretation. This is the more likely because the tabernacle as well as the temple made use of the services of men who were proficient in the plastic arts, even (think of Bezaleel and Aholiab, who are given a prominent place in Dr. Abraham Kuyper's concept of common grace) by divine appointment. Nevertheless, "Jesus" has not given any direct instructions regarding, say, a theory of art, which, in whatever way one may wish to answer the question that was asked above, would at any rate have been fitting there. When one thinks of the man Jesus as the chief Prophet and Teacher, also for the artist, of Him Who lived always in the presence of God without sin, then His "attitude" in this respect will be the more "disappointing," at least for those who would like to hear from the mouth of "Jesus" a more or less developed system of cultural ethics or aesthetics. Even the (developed) prolegomena are lacking in "His" teachings. He did not teach His "own" ideas: He was not a lecturer but a Prophet. How often did He not say: "It is written"? Speaking this way He does not take His place behind a lectern to teach a system that carries His own name, but He takes His place among all the prophets; and even when He shows Himself to be more than these, as their "fulfilment," He can never be separated from them. This is most "disappointing"; this "Jesus" considers it an honour that no lectures on His "own" rules are to be expected from Him. He came, as He says, not to destroy the God-given "Law" (*torah*) but to fulfil it. "To fulfil" is not the same as "to destroy" (by means of His "own" system), and also not the same as "to add unto."

Above we mentioned the absence of a fully developed and direct *thetic* theory of culture. However, does "Jesus" perhaps present a kind of polemics or apologetics regarding cultural theory? Or principles of stylistics? Or fragments thereof? Or aphorisms?

Quite easily one could encourage the notion that there was, after all. some reason for such during the period which He spent here below among men. We have here in mind the increasing hellenization of Israel's life in those days. Also the arts were greatly influenced by Hellenism. For example. music. Just as for the "sacred" *cult*-activities the Hebrew language obstinately maintained itself while Greek made itself felt in matters of *culture*, so Jewish music continued to be binding for the liturgist for use in the temple cult. but outside it the "free" hellenistic music fought against the Israelite style for predominance in profane-cultural use. Architecture showed the influence of several cultural phases but in particular of the hellenistic one and more and more lacked a character of its own. The public games. the governmental machinery. military service. fashion to some extent. they all were more or less patterned after foreign models. This, again. must have hurt from all sides the mind of the man Jesus. a mind sharpened with precision by the knives of the Law of God. A lack of style and in particular a loss of style must have wounded Him Who as a man happens to be God's second and supreme composition without flaw. It must always have struck Him. To Him as Bible-reader. by day and by night. a (not only *ahnend* but) Self-conscious Prophet. the levelling. the internationalization. the quasi-ecumenically interested denaturalization of (also) the cultural life of His people — a denaturalization which in fact prostituted itself to all the "gentiles" — must have been to Him a pressing reason for anxiety. For partly this was one of the consequences of the dispersion of Abraham's children among the nations. And was this dispersion not called God's *judgment*? It showed the vestiges, the traces or remnants. of the mastery of foreign powers that had successively overrun the people of "Jesus." In this dispersion He saw the results of Israel's sin; and *only in the second place* He saw in it a preparation for His own mission. Israel's dependence on other countries was to Him a matter of punishment. In it He distinguished sin, loss, weakness, worldliness. And is not sin the most severe punishment of sin? This is how already the prophet Zephaniah had seen things. For this prophet, too, had fulminated against a raving about, e.g., foreign fashions or against a copying of foreign customs ("leaping on the threshold," Zephaniah 1:8, 9). During King Josiah's reformation he had joined the battle against the sin of ogling demagogues and fulminated against "acting the Assyrian way" — just as still today among us the "stalwart" Calvinist, at least in theory, discerns a bad odour in the fashion of Paris, and the puritan is on the alert against any possible infiltration by a cultural "fifth column." For the company of exotic drill-sergeants deserves no gentler name. The one prophet fulminates against populations the youth of which speaks "half in the speech of Ashdod" (Nehemiah 13:24); the other calls for the days when there will no longer be a "Canaanite" (such a huckster) pottering about in the temple of Yahweh. Philistine influences are broken by the one reformer in the south, Syrian ones by the other in the north. The importing of foreign religions, at least their "forms" (as if these could be abstracted from their contents) for the sake of business relations and cultural contacts, is plainly called "going awhoring" by a third one. All the prophets know quite well that Israel is first of all "the Church" and only then "a nation." It is a nation only because it is the Church. And behold, after so many centuries there is now "Jesus," standing in the midst of His people, realizing He is the precursor-successor of Zephaniah, and of all the reformers, temple-purgers, and prophets, and still He does not produce for His "contemporaries" a detailed and fashionable system of hodogetics regarding "fashions" or their opposite; neither does He in a direct way lecture on style and cultural forms. But He preaches, leads, prays, holding His Bible in His hand and His fishermen by His hand. Even in the matter of the marriage problem He refuses to choose between the two theories presented to Him regarding the right of divorce (the doctrine of Hillel over against that of Shammai, Matthew 19). He never looked at a woman. What is all this? Is this negativism? Or asceticism? Is this a matter of surrendering riches of life which can surely be considered wealth? Is it a hankering after a *dôme des invalides*? Please stop asking questions. Rather realize that with our questions-with-no-answers we are sent from pillar to post as long as the full biblical light concerning the *Christ* has not dawned upon the doings of *Jesus*.

11. Therefore the problem is none other than "*Jesus the Christ* and culture."

For in this combination of the two names the key to its solution has been given us. Jesus: the *essence* of His office (to save, *pleromatically*). *The* Christ: the *legitimacy* of His office (He has been "ordained" of God, definitively) and also the *guarantee* of His office (He was anointed "with the Spirit," not with some ointment only, and consequently: He always attains what He definitively wants to attain in pleromatic respect). Those two names, which have been combined this way once only, exclusively, in this one Person-having-two-distinct-natures, create style in what seems to be stylelessness, and a chord out of the single tones. Now that in the light of the Scriptures we have seen these two names combined in *Him*, we hold the clue and are able to read the music of "the life of Jesus": *Ein wohltemperiertes Klavier*. Rather, not "a" but "the" Well-Tempered

Clavichord. For now the *office* of this Man of God requires our attention. And from the fulfilling of the *office* which He holds when awake and when asleep, in going and in sitting down, in speaking and in keeping silent, the preaching of the counsel of God concerning *Jesus Christ* comes to us.

This, then, applies to the first term of our problem. Moreover, from the fulfilling of the same office we get a clear insight also into the second term of our problem: *cultural* life, the cultural task, the concept of culture.

12. In the above we have time and again emphasized the fact that Jesus Christ cannot be known without the Scriptures — which He Himself used to quote in order to prove His identity. We had to put our finger at this detail because otherwise we would still not arrive where we would like to be. There have been hundreds of "Jesuses" (Joshuas). They are still there, in the ghettos and in the market places. Strictly speaking, there have also been millions of "christs" (anointed ones) and they are still there, in catacombs and fortunately also on the city squares. However, as for the son of Mary and Joseph (as was supposed), the fact that He would deserve to be called Jesus (Joshua) truly and exhaustively and that in Him the divine appointment would be definitive and His being enabled to fulfil His task adequate, this we do not know from the sound of the names, neither do we read this in His parousia, His appearance, but we *hear* this from the Scriptures.

And now that we know all this, we see that, although His *office* never separates the Christ of the Scriptures from the people and in so far does not isolate or abstract Him from them, nevertheless His unique and exhaustive, definitive, and pleromatic anointing, and this connected with His unique Person (constituted of two distinct natures), made Him as the second Adam and as a Mediator entirely different in all His work from anyone else. His work, since it was and is the work belonging to His *office*, is seeking us all. But because it was and is *His* work, it always defines Him in His unique service to God. One cannot copy Him without underrating Him. There are thousands of soldiers, but there is only one generalissimo. Whoever wants to have this one generalissimo imitated, paralyzes the whole army. The generalissimo is closely connected with them all, and he decides for everyone what the regulation uniform will be, but he himself is "non-regulation." However, the law of the country has been written into his heart. *Law* and *uniform* are two different things.

Let us again take up the thread of our argument: Not to get married was a command for Him alone. His office was to suffer and die. His office consisted of a struggle against God and against Satan at the turning-point of the ages. His office was: to be the second Adam; that is, to establish a community of men, this time not of one blood, as a living soul, but from one Spirit as a quickening *pneuma*. It commissions Him to rule over a large nation, not because this nation has in common the same strongly beating blood nor a common struggle and triumph, but on the judicial ground of the unique sacrifice of the blood that flowed forth only from *His* broken body.

This office put Him among men, as One Who was never authorized to isolate Himself but Who yet was completely lonely in the *idion* of His "experience" (His peculiar experience). For "experience" means: to experience that the Word which God spoke concerning us comes true. Well, then, a very peculiar Word was spoken regarding Him, a Word relevant to His unique situation. Only by enduring this loneliness He could presently praise God and cause Him to be praised by a great multitude. This office engulfed Him, even bodily. It totally obligated Him. It so completely dominated His spiritual and bodily life that all His flesh and blood devoted itself fully to the one great battle that He would wage in righteousness and strength before God (*enōpion Theou, coram Deo*). Who does not immediately feel that with this everything has in principle been said about Jesus' status as an unmarried Person? Who does not feel that He would even have been unable to "heal" marriage, also as a cultural monument, if He, as the Servant of the LORD, had not taken upon Himself His yoke, without co- or adoption of "the children given to Him" according to the law of flesh and blood? "Forasmuch then as the children are partakers of flesh and blood, He also Himself likewise took part of the same" (Hebrews 2:14). For He is not ashamed to call Himself "the Brother of us all." This is His office. However, He would have been ashamed indeed to call Himself the (physical) Father of some of us. FOR THIS IS NOT HIS OFFICE. His unmarried state is not a pattern for us, nor a humiliatingly "high" ideal for the man who has not the charisma of abstinence. His *office* is so different.

One who has seen this office will presently know what to think about all those other details which we have mentioned above as being all riddles. The gold of the Magi from the East, e.g., and their gifts of incense and myrrh had only to serve the Great Commission. The costly ointment, the woven garment, the fine table in the house of prominent people — they all had to serve the fulfilling of His *office*. To be sure, He had no place to lay down His head, but this was no proof of contempt of culture, neither was it a silent protest against dwelling in ceiled houses "as such," for the prophets did not curse the dwelling in ceiled houses but only the sin of those who were dwelling in them and at the same time neglected the temple. No, it was a cause of necessary sorrow in His struggle to *give* us real culture, among other things; in this battle His God never lets Him go "on leave." He selected His fishermen, people of all kinds, not as if, sociologically speaking, only the poor and unpretentious in the cultural world could please Him (besides, they were not so "poor," those Galileans), but because He had to work also among the people of Galilee; and further, He did not chose fishermen only or Galileans exclusively. Did He take them from among the poor? The one says He did, the other remembers just in time that some of them left behind a business: they were, in this case, no poor devils who squinted with envy at the golden ornaments of the ladies of Jerusalem, but determined heroes who had given up the "gold-mine" of their business: the prophecy concerning the Messiah had caused their heart to burn within them. Christ selected those people for the apostolate because He wanted them to preach that the gold may again adorn the chair of the prominent ones if this chair has been built not on the foundation of what makes one great among men, but of that which is right before God. In this selection of apostles, then, He was on His way to the hour of revelation when He would cast down all the cultural philosophers with that fine and decisive word of revelation: "the fine linen" of the most beautiful city "is the righteousness of the saints" (Revelation 19:8). The establishing of leper-houses will surely follow if only first of all justice and the concept of the office, which forbids euthanasia, are again acknowledged in accordance with the written law of God. Even the Law of Moses already knew all about social service — the isolation of lepers included. However, Moses considered this as a matter of *theocratic* service in and to the Church, on covenant territory. Thus Christ does not give leper-houses but He gives them *back*, even when the covenant territory is no longer geographically the same as under Moses, but can presently be distinguished in *local Churches*. He wants to have a royal crown, but only when the crown of thorns has obtained it. He transforms His fishermen into preachers, and His preachers into organizers of, e.g., a movement for the abolition of slavery, but first the world must be told that the most serious and most painful and most humiliating slavery is that of sin, and the basis of this essential slavery must be taken out of the life of the world by *His* humbling Himself unto death, His having become a slave (Philippians 2). He, then, knows with the certainty and practicality of a seer the times and hours of His office. For this reason He, for example, sometimes on purpose leaves some sick people in their sickness.

While He healed others, He passes them by, but He does so because He leaves them to be healed by the charismatic power of His apostles. Therein He wants to show, that, as often as these apostles of His heal sick people after Pentecost, He Himself, with His Spirit, has in them come back to this world, still being alive after He has died. But who will ever see this leaving of sick people in their sickness (e.g., that drudge at the gate of the temple called Beautiful) in *this* light, if "Jesus" has not become to him *Christ*, the Christ Whose "being a seer" is accompanied by prophecy?

Yes, indeed, He wants to be understood as the *Christ of the Scriptures*, also in order to be able to give us insight into His positive attitude towards the problems which we touched on under number 10, above. He shall speak either directly or indirectly, and fundamentally, about architecture, the plastic arts, music, fashions, about the struggle between the tendency to level the cultural development of a nation and the urge to maintain its specific character. However, He shall do so only as *Christ*, as the One Who as the uncreate, eternal Logos, even before the birth of "Jesus," dominated the history and culture of all the nations, and Who on the feast of Pentecost entered into His working period of "a thousand years" from Ascension Day and Pentecost until His second coming. In this final period of the everlasting, now incarnate Word of God, He shall complete and perfect His work as the Christ — in every respect, also in that of the questions and struggles regarding the "cultures" of the past,' the present, and the future; and, moreover, also by establishing a *Christian culture* in the midst of the world.

13. Further, also with respect to the second term of our problem, that is, for the development of the concept of "culture" or "cultural life" which is in full harmony with God's revelation, the Scriptural concept of the office is of direct and constituent significance. Only when we take into account the office concept, as it was grasped so well especially by John Calvin, there will be an end to the tiresome game of the spirits, of which the one plays "religion" off against "culture," the other "culture" against "religion."

The chain of thought is here readily handed to us.

As for the "second" Adam, we must go back to the *beginning* of things, when the "first one" was there, the first one to whom God, Who gave revelation within the communion of His covenant, also made known the first *principles* of it. For the first Adam was — at least for those who do not think in an evolutionistic way — not a child, no playfully naive person. To use the language of the Belgic Confession of Faith, he did indeed, together with all other creatures, have his *officium*, His task as part of the created unity of God's works. However, for him — just as for the angels — the *officium* became an *office*. He had been made by God in order to be an office-bearer, not just as part of the huge world-engine, but also as the engine-driver appointed by God, and answerable to Him, answerable not in the first but in the second capacity.

This appointment of *adam* (man) to such a responsible office determines his whole course of action in all his relationships. It even determines his qualities. For God created him just as He wanted him to be. And God wanted him to be a purposeful office-bearer. From this point of view the concept of the "naive" primitive man disappears completely. Man is given the title of "God's fellow-worker."[5] He is given His own work in such a wide cosmic context that in the original world of paradisal purity this work can immediately and always be called "liturgy"; that is, service in and to the Kingdom. To which Kingdom? To the one of which God is King; that is, the Kingdom of heaven, the subjects of which have been distributed over two sections of the cosmos: one "upper" section and one "lower" section. If this is the image of the first Adam, then the Christ can justly bear the name of the second Adam only if He, too — as man — falls within and wants to fall within the framework of these categories of office. For it is precisely as the second Adam that the Christ as office-bearer in the *middle* of history must revert to its *beginning* and to the then given *principles*. By fulfilling His office — which is fundamentally the same as that of all men — before God's countenance, He takes upon Himself the great reformational task of *returning to the ABC*[6] of world and life order. To serve God, in concrete life, to obey God in any function, to fulfil God's expressed will with all that is in us and to do so in the midst of and in organic relation and communion with all that is around us — *this is the ABC*. Here the problem of *culture*, and also its definition, has been stated in principle.

Presently we shall come back to this point.

But when after having provisionally looked for a resting-point for our thoughts, we take up the thread again, then we see Christ in His *office* standing in the midst of world history. It is in such a way that the concept of the "midst of history" (Tillich et al.) is developed in accordance with the Scriptures. It is no "category," on the same level with the "border concept" of a so-called a-historical "beginning" or with that of an equally a-historical "*eschaton*" — again taken as a "border concept" — but it is a result of a real measuring and dividing of time into real periods of time. There is indeed a historical *beginning*; then it was that man was created and that he *fell* into sin. There will also be an *end*: when everyone will receive the things done "in his body" (by him in his temporal existence here below) (II Corinthians 5:10). So the "middle" of history is the period in which Christ comes to redeem this end from the curse of being exclusively determined by the fall and rupture that took place so shortly after the beginning.

**14.** For, to make it again possible for man to fulfil this original service of God, and to give back to Him His world and His work-community, Christ comes to do two things.

In the first place He comes to reconcile God and to still His wrath. He does this in perfect alliance with God Himself, Who is the subject of the *"katallagē"* (reconciliation): "God was in Christ reconciling the world unto Himself" (II Corinthians 5:19). "In Christ" He was the only Author of this *katallagē*. For the eternally burning hatred of God against all sin cannot keep its postulates in harmony with those of His eternally flaming mercy unless during time (in the so-called middle of history) God's *punishing* as well as His *demanding* justice is satisfied. The punishing justice requires the complete condemnation of the guilty one; the demanding justice still desires the rendering of an inviolate obedience "in the body" (that is, during a man's lifetime). Therefore the Christ stands surety with respect to this twofold justice. And He indeed fulfils the pledge. This way He within time brings about the judicial verdict that was known and demanded by God's wrath as well as by His love; with the ransom of His blood He purchases the right of the renewal of what is now called God's "new" mankind. It is now called His redeemed Christian congregation, which through Him and together with Him is heir to eternal life.

However, since for Him and for all people this eternal life — like eternal death — began and shall begin already here, in this "cultural world," He does yet a second thing. All life and death is now given to Him to be administered by Him, because they remain determined in their everlasting character by the judicially-constituent ransom of Himself in the "middle of history." This way He administers eternal death as Christ's sentence-of-condemnation to those who have alienated themselves in their historical existence from His judicial verdict ("whereunto also they were appointed," I Peter 2:8). Consequently through His Holy Spirit (Who actively propels the "middle of history" towards the "end") He is coming to do two things. On the one hand He will, in the cultural world, cause the grapes of the earth to ripen in order to be trodden in the winepress of the administration of God's anger. On the other hand He comes, through the same Holy Spirit, "in" Whom He Himself "completes" the "thousands years" of His own dominion of peace, to equip the work-and-office community of God which He Himself purchased for the work and service of God, in order that all its living members may enter into the city of perfect glory.

It is a struggle of a *judicial* nature.

For that reason it is also a struggle for *power*.

The *judicial* struggle which He fought before God and Satan was decided in the middle of the history of the world and that way He put it again on a firm foundation.

And the *dynamic* battle, which in principle He won for ever, brings for God's newly-purchased work-community, the *new mankind*, which is nevertheless fundamentally the same as "the old," great powers of the outpouring of the Spirit, powers of sanctification, of Church conquest, of world maturation, of cultural action.

This twofold fulfilling of His office renders transparent for us Christ's life as an office-bearer here below and in heaven and is of predominant significance for the problem under consideration.

**15.** For in the fulfilling of this office, whereto He has been called and also perfectly equipped, this corrupt world experiences once again the miracle of the appearance of the whole, the beautiful, the original or, if one wants, the "ideal" man. As long as He is in the state of humiliation this wholeness and pureness is only there in concealment. Then it is the decorum of a pure, sinless human nature that always responds to God's timely speaking in faithfulness to His Law. However, then it has not yet gained its reward, which glorifies Him also externally, rendering immortality to His human nature. The reward that glorifies Him also publicly is given Him in the state of glorification: He has become now a King-in-His-beauties. Psalm 110:3 is always fulfilled in Him: and many a cultural philosopher would like to have written these fine words as soon as he had understood them.

The whole man, is he presented as a gift? Yes, he is. For (a) Christ is the whole man, standing in our midst; wherefore He can say: The Kingdom of God is "in your midst." This flawless man did not turn His back to the others, not even for a single moment. And not only this, but (b) by the almighty power of the Spirit given to Him, He also creates a man who in principle is whole again, as a fruit of creative regeneration.

To believe this, has its consequences.

*Ad a:* Since cultural achievements are among man's mandates, and since no one can act in such a way that his actions have no cultural significance, Christ, the sinless One, is the only One Who in an entirely pure manner has acted and is still acting upon cultural life. That is to say, He is the only One among men-after-the-Fall. Who can comprehend the fulness of the thoughts, also the cultural thoughts, that are included in the dogma of the Church that sees and preaches Christ as Man-without-sin? As the sinless One He responds, in words and deeds, in a way that is always entirely to the point in every situation into which the Spirit thrusts Him in order that He should prove Himself to be the second Adam, even in a world that in cultural respect is far removed from that of the first Adam. What is a more direct cultural act than to react to cultural situations and complications fully and purely, and fundamentally, and according to the original rule? And in all this He is not just "a" man, but the Son of man. That is to say: He is more than a bright spot or a ray of light for a world that, also in cultural respect, is heading for the abyss; He is the *Sun* of righteousness, also in this respect. "Sun" does not only mean a source of light but also a source of energy. As the Logos-Mediator-Surety He is the hypostasis, the solid foundation, the original ground, the fulfiller, redeemer, and renewer of culture — a cultural sign which shall therefore be spoken against.

*Ad b*: And because He as the Messiah, even before appearing under the name of Jesus, and also afterwards — that is, all through the centuries — takes action by virtue of the *right* to be obtained or already obtained in the middle of history, by His redeeming *power*, He makes certain people again as they were "in the beginning": men of God. In the midst of a "crooked and perverse generation" He places the types of a humanity that is in principle pure. They are not perfect yet; however, in principle they *are* there again. They are there from the very moment when Adam in faith submits himself to the Word of the first Gospel promise. And they continue to appear, they increase, they become "the great multitude which no man could number," the multitude of those who in Christ have been sanctified by the Spirit. Their host is increasing in number and is always to be counted, until the last day.

In this administration of His own office, and in the formation of those who are anointed together with Him ("Christians") there comes about nothing less than a divine action (an action proceeding from the Father, the Son, and the Spirit) to conquer the world for God, by the Christ of God. "The earth is the LORD's, and the fulness thereof" (Psalm 24:1). This conquest is a re-conquest: the property is, as far as it has been destined from eternity, brought back to and restored in its proper relation to the Owner. Christ connects the beginnings of the world with the end, the earliest history with that of the last days, the first things with the *eschata*, alpha with omega, the

35

ABC of God's efficacious legislative Word of the beginning with the XYZ of His once again efficacious evangelical Word at the end of time. For God's legislative speaking in the beginning of the world — to undefiled Adam — was a matter of speaking in, and on the basis of, the *covenant*: a matter of ordering the mutual relation between God and man, in promise and in demand. This covenant together with its ordinances had then to govern the world from the beginning to the end. And now that, after the breaking of the covenant by the first Adam, the second Adam goes in the way of the covenant again, and restores the same, now the end will still be there as yet, in peace, but this is the *pax Christi* — otherwise there is no peace at all. This way Christ brings all that is in the world to its consummation: that which is secular and that which is ecclesiastical, the seed of the woman and the seed of the serpent, the power of angels and the brute force of demons. He went before us and then, together with us, back to the origins of God's creation. He there read from the Law tables the work rules which God in the beginning had imposed upon the man of God: that in the history of the created world any labourer created by God had to trace in himself all the "talents" which God had distributed to His labourers in the morning of creation, and learn to use them in such a way that finally, by making productive the "possibilities" which had been put into the creation and afterwards had to be discovered and respected according to their "kind," man would exploit all its potentials. All the talents which the Master had given to His servants were to have gained in the end, in the evening, as many as were distributed in the morning. And all the possibilities hidden in the cosmos had to be traced, discovered, made to function according to the revealed law, and rendered subservient to the edification of the whole of God's creation according to the order of the respective creatures that had been established from the beginning. If the personal man — assisted in this respect by the other personal office-bearer created by God, the angel — were to fulfil his '*munus*' (office) this way, then, to use an expression taken from the Belgic Confession of Faith, any non-personal creature, and also man — and angel — himself, would fulfil again his *officium* (office, or service) (Article 12). This is, if one wants to put it that way, the *Theocratic* arrangement of all things.

No less than this did Christ find written in the order of the day which God inscribed in the heart of the cultural man of the beginning, the flawless man in the beautiful garden without a gate called "The Beautiful," for the garden was open then.

What He read there so laid hold of and dominated Him that — just to give an example — as appears from the synoptic Gospels, He told the parable of the *talents*, wherein this ABC is taught again — for *reforming* means: to teach the people the ABC again — as the last one before He, in accordance with His office, went the way of His sufferings and resurrection. It was the last one He told before His "Millennium" broke through. It so laid hold of Him that in His last great prayer for the Church, "sent up" in the days of His humiliation, He told the Father: "I pray not that Thou shouldest take them out of the world, but that Thou shouldest keep them from the evil" (John 17:15), that Thou shouldest keep them there, not in their cloister, which becomes a refuge of self-willed religion, a refectory of fatigue, at least if it has no window and no door open to the world.

16. This last point, the ABC of the first days of the world, is the turning-point in our argument. At this very moment the door is put on its hinges, and it must fit. And — here alone *can* it fit.

For here alone we come to the possibility of working out the above-given, still only provisional, concept of culture. For culture is a word that can be found on the first page of the Bible: "Dress the garden, replenish the earth, be fruitful and multiply" (Genesis 2:15; 1:28). These first Bible-pages, they are the pages of "the ABC." They contain these three brief commandments in the description of the phase of the so-called "covenant of works." They already fit in the virgin world *which has not yet been completed*; that is, which is still in the process of being developed — according to the plan of creation — in order to reach the end, the *teleiōsis*, the entering into the state of being fullgrown. Therefore this first page of the Bible, replete as it is with covenant regulations, is directly of cultural interest. For the Creator Himself is culturally interested. "Culture," after all, is a word that has been derived from the Latin verb *colere*. *Colere* means "to cultivate," "to care for." The farmer who plows his field is engaged in this *colere*. There is a field, which is a promise. And there is seed, which is also a promise. But there is also a farmer, which means: "a *commandment* with a *promise*." As a creature of God he has been put in a cosmic unity together with the field and the seed. He himself is also a "field" of the everlasting Spirit, and at the same time he is seed. He, too, is in his entire bodily existence a creature of God's hand, his "conscience," his consciousness, included. As a creature of God he, too, is included when the Belgic Confession of Faith states that all creatures are as so many characters in a most elegant book (Article 2). But God placed him as a personal creature not only *in* but also *over* all other created life. That is to say, man is, with his conscience, not only a *character* in the book of creation but also a *reader* of this "book": he must read and understand also himself as a character, although never isolating himself from other creatures. *Deum scire cupio, et animam*: I desire to know God *and* the soul. This well-known saying means, as far as this "soul," known through God, is concerned, that it — or let us say: the conscience, conscious life — is a character in but also a reader of God's book. So man as a personal-spiritual being, as a called labourer of God, and as the crowned vice-regent, by the finding and sowing of all seed is to take from the field what is in it. It is *agri-culture*.

However, in order to fulfil this task, as a lord of this field, and also, though as a personal being, to confess that he (he consciously) is one with this field, under God, he must undertake self-cultivation. This self-cultivation immediately finds its limits here. It may not be or even be called "personalism." As soon as the "person" is considered as "divine," or (which is fundamentally the same thing) as an end in itself, as a reader who no longer wants to be a character in the book of God, he has fallen to the share of idolatry, the idolatry of "person cultivation." He then forgets that in "the book" of creation *God's* name is to be read, and that the God Who may be known from this book as the Creator and Re-creator is transcendent, to an infinite degree qualitatively distinct from all creatures. Self-cultivation, self-development, this *positive (!) askēsis*, that is, the training of the creaturely aspect in us, in order that what is human and creaturely may find its *officium* herein that man as a creature may see his *munus* and fulfil it — this is good and even commanded. His hand shall sow and deposit the seed in the field of the world. He shall be the medium by which, in faith and faithfulness to the promises which God spoke to His fellow-workers, the silent promises that God put into His creatures, each in its own context, shall find their appropriate fulfilment. In such a self-development, such a self-cultivation, he prepares himself for the growing task, and he lets his God take pleasure also in himself as active field.

This was God's wise intent when He created the world. It did not please Him to create the world ready to hand. He only created it good. The world, then, as it came forth from God's hands, was a world-in-the-promise, a world-in-hope; and as long as it was good this hope could not be called "idle." Neither will the ordinances of creation, those fixed "laws," ever be invalid, "powerless" (unto our perfection) "unless through the flesh." That is to say, when sin makes its entrance. Not that sin can push aside the ordinances of creation. Definitely not. Their continuity is the first condition for the blessing as well as for the curse — both of which were already announced in paradise. However, the ordinances of creation, which in an obedient world always make the blessing concrete and multiply it, will do the same in a fallen world as far as the curse is concerned. Then they are "powerless" unto blessing, but not unto cursing.

This is how God immediately spoke in the sanctions of His "covenant of works," and in so doing He put the whole world, man in particular, under high pressure, under "tension." For man, called as a fellow-worker of (and also under) God, the world was not a world of the "omega" but of the "alpha." The paradisal world was a beginning. And in this beginning was given, in principle, everything that had to be there potentially to let it grow out to a completed world of perfect order, the *polis*, the *civitas*, the "city" (state) of God, paradisally designed and presently built. If one day it is to be full-grown, it needs a historical process of many centuries. We are indeed in an "interim"; but it lies not between a primitive and an eschatological "history," both of which would be *a-historical*, but between the "first" and the "last" things, which are as *historical* as the things in "the middle of history." Otherwise it would be nonsense to speak of a "middle." The paradisal reality, then, is definitely not a so-called "higher" reality; neither is Adam. It is only a *virginal* reality; but for the rest it is, very concretely, included in time, sober, real, historical; there is flesh in it, and blood, just as there are soul and spirit. And Spirit.

And now, in this sober, flat reality of historical paradisal life, God announced that He would work *evolution* on the foundation of *creation*. This evolution, according to the nature of created life, cannot take place without the energy which flows out from God, not even for one moment. But, according to God's own commanding Word, which creates order and allots to everything is own place, it should not happen, not even for one single moment, without man as man-of-God acting therein as God's fellow-worker. "You are labourers together with God" (I Corinthians 3:9); this is not a posthumous *quietive* that was proclaimed by Paul for a seceded Church somewhere in an isolated corner. No, this is a matter of leading back in an *imperative* way to the "*first principles* of the world." This is not only a suitable text for a minister's inaugural sermon, but it is also the day-text for any cultural worker, for the professor as well as the street-sweeper, for the kitchen-worker and for the composer of a Moonlight Sonata.

Therefore the first commandment with a rich promise reads: "Dress the garden." No castles in the air are promised in these words; neither do they suggest a so-called "higher reality." Dress the garden — here first of all the spade, a cultural instrument, and later on rubberboots, are not put into our hands, but man's created spirit has to *invent* them according to time and place and to design and adapt them to the dressing hand and the foot that breaks up and tramples down the soil. For the hand and the spirit, they work together: *man* has to "dress." Dress the garden — here no introspective moralizing sermons are delivered, but here there is a concrete work- and life-commandment, a highly-spiritual and, consequently, everyday commandment. Biblical interim ethics can only operate with a *lex* that can be grasped. A "commandment" that one cannot lay hold of, a Word of God that one cannot work with, would not enable it to fulfil its pedagogic calling of prescription. For the garden may be called "paradise," and our lyrical rhetoric unfortunately may have changed it as if by magic into an isolated, solidly fenced-in spot, where zephyrs blow and which, its seems, only a popularly-misunderstood romanticism can write about. But actually it is something completely different. The garden is the beginning of *adama*, of the inhabited world. Hence it is also the beginning of the cultural world. The garden lies open. Therefore we earlier spoke about the beautiful garden but one without a gate called "The Beautiful." All that which issues from the world issues from there, including that which issues from cultural life and all its processes. For CULTURE becomes HERE (!) THE SYSTEMATIC ENDEAVOUR TOWARDS THE PROCESS-WISE ACQUISITION OF THE AGGREGATE OF LABOUR BY THE SUM-TOTAL OF HUMAN BEINGS AS THEY BELONG TO GOD, EVOLVE THEMSELVES UNTO GOD IN HISTORY WITH AND FOR THE COSMOS, AND ARE PRESENT AT ANY HISTORICAL MOMENT, HAVING ASSUMED THE TASK OF DISCLOSING THE POTENCIES LYING DORMANT IN CREATION AND SUCCESSIVELY COMING WITHIN REACH IN THE COURSE OF THE HISTORY OF THE WORLD, OF DEVELOPING THEM IN COMPLIANCE WITH THEIR INDIVIDUAL NATURES, OF MAKING THEM SUBSERVIENT TO THEIR ENVIRONMENT, BOTH FAR AND NEAR, ACCORDING TO THEIR COSMIC RELATIONSHIPS AND IN SUBMISSION TO THE NORMS OF GOD'S REVEALED TRUTH; AND ALL THIS IN ORDER TO MAKE THE TREASURES THUS ACQUIRED USABLE BY MAN AS LITURGICAL CREATURE, AND, SUBSEQUENTLY, TO BRING THEM, TOGETHER WITH THE NOW MORE THOROUGHLY EQUIPPED MAN HIMSELF, BEFORE GOD AND PUT THEM AT HIS FEET, IN ORDER THAT HE MAY BE ALL IN ALL, AND EVERY WORK MAY PRAISE ITS MASTER.

In this definition the fundamental moments of the biblical creation story have, in our opinion, been rendered. *Dress the garden*: the concrete cultural mandate to exploit the world's potentials. *Be fruitful and multiply*: a growing sum-total of human beings to be subjected to the cultural mandate, the obligation to engage in culture, time and again in every temporal phase and in all provinces of geographic space. *Subdue the earth, and have dominion*: the cultural man, as a product of God's creation work, facing his own position: that of God's vice-regent. *Man created in God's own image*: cultural work must be spontaneous (man's qualities have been created in him in view of his *munus*); it is a matter of serving God as a representative of His supreme authority and consequently a matter of discovering God and causing Him to be found in the discovering of the future. God speaks *unto man and with him*, because of his appointment as the chosen representative of God's dominion over all other creatures; and within the communion of the covenant that God made with him, God speaks unto him and with him about the rest of the cosmos in spite of the fact that he himself is part thereof — which means that self-distinction is thus awakened in him, and that self-cultivation, self-development is made clear to him as his duty, not as an end in itself but as a matter of mandate. And finally, he is given a *moral* commandment: together with all that belongs to him he is in his cultural labour subject to his Creator: in the determining of his own goals with regard to created things he is bound to what he has heard from God's mouth by Word-revelation concerning God's own purpose with respect to the cosmos. He is summoned to kneel down, now and presently, before his Maker in and together with a cosmos prepared by his own hand under God's providence, culturally engaged as he is in view of his own, but especially of God's *sabbath*, into which he, man, has to enter.

Under the influence of thinking that has been corrupted by sin and is hostile to God, in a world that disrupts all relationships, culture is usually separated from "religion," or at least sharply distinguished from it. *But from the beginning it was not so* (Matthew 19:8). For religion is not a province of life, not a separate function of or for the "heart," not an isolated activity of a devout conventicle of people during certain elevated fragments of man's lifetime. No, religion, or rather, the service of God, is to be distinguished from religiosity. Schleiermacher, the pantheistic philosopher-in-the-guise-of-a-theologian of Romanticism, wrote a book entitled *On Religion*. However, he dealt only with religiosity and at bottom — by virtue of his pantheism — this religiosity was self-worship, in so far as "God" and "universe" are intertwined in his thinking. He of necessity had to reject as moralism any action having an objective. "Religion" was to him neither a matter of "doing" nor of "knowing." In our interpretation it is no mere "doing" either. It is *service*; however, not that of an all-nature particle oscillating together with the universe, a particle called *homunculus*, but the service of the man who loves his Father, knows Him as being *above* the world, believes Him *in the* world, and wants to turn again *to Him* with the world, in order that he may consciously — not by deriving all sorts of "formulas" from the "universe" but by listening to *commandments*-of-instruction from the mouth of his Father-Legislator — formulate his maxims in the believing "knowledge" of the Church, and so fulfil the will of his Father. For this reason cultural work is in paradise *service of God*. There one cultivates everything, the ground on which one walks and the heart in its full depth, plants as well as the meditative spirit. There one washes his undefiled hands as well as his soul in righteousness — the one thing cannot be separated from the other.

And culture will take its God-appointed place again only there where one reaches back to this original situation and its order.

**17.** We said, *reaches back*. This expression already includes the confession that there was a disruption.

This disruption was caused by sin; man fell away from God.

Then there was disintegration. His life crumbled. The same happened to the world: the whole of it and its respective parts did no longer work towards each other. The human mind, confused, erring, sinful, conceited, itself disintegrated in principle, began to practise disintegration, that is, to abstract, to tear asunder, to set apart and separate. Man ceased to think in a general and widely-cosmic way, keeping the "parts" in a proper relation to "the whole" and putting all this under God's feet, but he changed his "catholicizing" interest to a "specializing," that is, detailing interest. Details, which one can become enamoured of, were severed from the "whole," in which one must love God. He stopped his ears to the truth revealed to him in God's Law and confirmed by the tragic failures of his existence, the truth that he, once he had fallen into sin, could or would no longer survey any single theme in the great context of the whole of God's compositions, let alone that he could or would work it out in his own.

This is how religion and culture were separated from one another: the vanguard of the generation of Cain chose "culture" and discarded "religion" as something unrelated; and the rear guard of the generation of Seth quite agreed with this distinction. And that was the worst thing. *For from the beginning it was not so.*

Sin worked still further destruction. For the process of disintegration cannot stop. Not only the abstracting severance of the whole into "parts," "spheres," "sectors," "territories," "groups with common interests," is by itself the result of sin, but even within these "spheres," "territories," "communities" themselves (existing as a result of abstraction) the factor of dissolution becomes further active to increase the effect of the de-catholicizing principle. For while God lets the *distinctions* which He has put into His creation combine unto and in a "pluriform"' *unity*, Satan makes use of these distinctions to *separate* things. God binds the respective races together and shows in their coalescence mankind's "pluriformity." Satan makes them principles of division, and so forces a racial struggle. It goes the same way as far as the different classes, sexes, characters, nationalities, and trade organizations are concerned. To use Pauline imagery again: eye cultivates eye, ear cultivates ear, hand cultivates hand, foot cultivates foot, and this rage of specialization eats its way so deeply that the question whether these respective parts of the body need each other, is reserved only for the moments when the world has a hangover, for example in what is called a post-war mentality. Even in these moments, asking the question is no more than a token vote. Personal aptitude is deformed into one-sidedness. One "type" will presently be the opposite of the other, of which it originally was to be only a complement. Everywhere differences become antitheses. Culture, as the systematic endeavour of the developing sum-total of human beings towards the acquisition of the aggregate of labour, is hereby already formally dissolving itself. For by acting this way people attack the system: the confusion of tongues is a matter of punishment, but it is then promptly presented as a good thing. This formal dissolution is the fruit of a material falling away from God. *Faith* in His covenant word was forsaken. The idea of man's office was thereby abandoned. Earnestness gave way to play, and to play-culture (sport-infatuation, four columns of sport reviews to half a column of Church news; big capitals for the winner of a match, but not a single letter for the cause of spiritual struggle, even in "Christian" newspapers). The *hope*, which in the regeneration of all things sees every part again in its proper place in the whole, has been forsaken; every day the world becomes more nervous and "culture" more and more a casemate business: everyone creeps into his own casemate at the command of "his" trade organization. *Love for God*, Who must be shown in His full glory in that which is His own, yields and gives way to infatuation with a creature that has broken away from its Maker. There is no unity any more. It is no longer even sought, because unity is found only through God, and God is considered an enemy. No longer the original style of the "commandment of life" (in paradise) is followed. And the reason which is given — if a reason is still given — is this: Well, we are in the desert now, and there one cannot do much with paradisal commandments. But this argument betrays the hypocrisy of those who use it: the law of life is held in contempt because God, Who by and in His Law gave life, is Himself denied. On his part, man broken away from God no longer has a cultural style that is determined by the moral law. Only in so far as God (as He presently will appear to be doing), for His own sake, yet keeps the created world within the natural context of the cosmos, man will feel himself to be bound by this fixed arrangement of God, also in his cultural achievements. Even though the *moral* law of God no longer determines man's cultural style, the *natural law* continues to bind the producer of culture with strong bonds. In the meantime the bonds of this natural coercion differ from the cords of God's love. The strong grip of God's *natural* ordinances enclasps God's friend as well as His enemy. But as far as this enemy is concerned, if it were up to him he would in his battle against the *moral* law try to avail himself of that which is *natural* and functions as such. If only he could, he would precisely in his immoral culture like to attain the proper "style" of Satan, who also has been unable to destroy the fundamental structure of God's original creation, but who yet desires to corrupt morally, with all his strength, the world given by God. There have already been some "cultural styles" of "Satanism."

18. As the foregoing implies, the mere fact that there is culture and that man performs cultural labour, cannot be classified under so-called "common grace."

This has indeed repeatedly been claimed. Taking the point of view of experience and at the same time making a "guided" effort to take biblical data into account, one then reasoned as follows: Because of the dreadful character of sin and guilt we, men, would have deserved to descend into hell immediately after the Fall. Such a descent, cutting off all development, would have served us right. Yet we see before our eyes that the world has continued to exist after the Fall for thousands of years, and that the potentialities given in the cosmos are being developed as yet. Is this not "grace"? The answer is then implied: It is indeed grace; it is God's goodness, which He does not owe to us. True, this grace does not redeem unto eternal salvation. Therefore it is called "common." Yet it is indeed "grace." It gives us the benefit of the *restraining* of sin. If sin were not restrained it would break out in the most flagrant, directly satanic outpouring of wickedness. However, God stems this wickedness by the "common" operation of His Spirit, even by the common "testimony" of the Spirit, which testimony provides man with certainty, the immediate assuredness concerning some clusters of central truths, this assuredness being pre-reflexive. In this way there falls upon the desert of this world the continually self-renewing dew of common grace, which makes life yet tolerable and even — by virtue of the "progressive" operation which is peculiar to it — creates oases in the midst of the desert, cultural oases also.

However, in this train of thought there are several twists which weaken the conclusion that the term "common grace" is applicable here.

Certainly, it is true that sin is being "restrained" and that the curse has not been fully poured out upon the world. However, the same thing can be said about the obedience which in Christ Jesus was again permitted to become a gift of God's free grace and which by the power of Christ's Spirit also was able to become a gift of this favour. Whoever calls the restraining of the curse "grace" should at least call the "restraining" of the blessing "judgment." But neither of these terms would have a scientific basis. As best they could be used in a non-scientific description of concrete reality, but then next to one another. However, this casual usage in speaking about "common grace" as well as "common judgment" means in itself already a correction of the preference for the term "common grace."

Certainly, there is a *withholding* (II Thessalonians 2:6). However, withholding is a feature peculiar to time. Where nothing is "withheld," there is a *possessio*[8] *tota simul* (a *possession* of life so that one always has the fulness of this possession simultaneously in his hands in *full* measure) OR a *privatio tota simul* (a matter of having been robbed, a deprivation, and then again in such a way that the fulness of this depravation is there *totally*, at every "moment" in full measure). That is to say: wherever there is no withholding, there is no temporal existence any longer; there "eternity" is found. For even in paradise there was a "withholding." If the Spirit of God had been given to Adam without a withholding, then he would have been excluded from the possibility of falling into sin. "Development" — or otherwise "corruption" — is a feature peculiar to time. Development and corruption belong to time. The *state* of being developed and being corrupted (both pleromatically, according to the subject's nature and capacity) belong to eternity. Consequently the fact that the gifts of creation show development is not grace, but *nature*. There is a stirring "within them," within things, within people. It is something "in" man: the boisterous urge of one who, since he is himself "developing," seeks to wrest corn and wine from the "developing" earth; that is, the urge to "*colere*," to *cultivate* the garden. However, that which before the Fall was a religious work of love, directed towards God as the Covenant God, becomes after the Fall a deed of selfishness, of self-preservation, of zest for living (a la *Pallieter*[9]), not service to God but self-service. One so often hears about "nature"

45

that one is left with the impression: this is dead capital lying there to be used or not to be used by man (and the world). Then one jumps to the conclusion: this world of man deserved to die, namely, to die an eternal death, which as such takes away from all its objects the possibility of any use of capital; yet man is able to "use" "nature," that is, to cause this dead capital still to yield interest; *ergo*, this is "grace."

But this reasoning is altogether faulty as long as "nature" is understood as temporal nature. As long as time exists, mobility, pregnancy and birth, begetting and conceiving, belong to nature. "Dead" capital — this is here too playful a terminology because it is not relevant to *nature-in-time* and because it only serves naively to distort the problem in order to be able to conclude that the term "common grace" is indeed applicable.

The problem under consideration, then, is fundamentally a matter of evaluating "time."

It is wrong to think that the prolongation of time after the Fall is a matter of "grace." One then refers us to the seriousness of sin, arguing that "we" deserved, immediately after the Fall, to be cast into the "lake of fire." This did not happen; *ergo*, it is grace. However, one forgets that the first sentence of this argument offers no more than a fable. If fallen man had been cast into the "lake of fire" immediately after the Fall, then "we" would not be there. Then only two people would have been condemned, and no more, no mankind, the subject of the just-mentioned hypothetical judgment.

Consequently a great mystery has been revealed precisely in the prolongation of time after the Fall. This prolongation is no grace. It is simple enough to "prove" this: Suppose God had intended to punish only as many people as he will indeed punish eternally, should these people then not have been born first, even successively, the one from the other? So God would have had to prolong time already for the purpose of casting into hell as many objects of His wrath as there will one day be. And not only this. During this time marriages would have had to be contracted; at any rate, the copulation of men and women would have had to occur. Therefore, e.g., an economic equilibrium would have been essential. Culture would have been necessary. Culture is the presupposition of all the works of God, even with respect to hell.

Praise be to God because we know more than only that there will be a hell. A heaven, too, is on the programme of divine action. In order to populate it with as many as God shall call thereunto, prolongation of time is needed, the bearing of children is essential, and consequently labour, in an economic as well as climatological equilibrium, is necessary. But precisely for that reason it is a serious error to designate the prolongation of time and the cultural development of the cosmos as (common) grace.

This prolongation and development are no grace. Nor are they curse or condemnation. That is to say, if one wants to use these terms in a serious way.

They are the *conditio sine qua non* of both, the substratum of both.

In so far as the urge to develop creation is natural, and in so far as the opening of any womb, even of that of mother earth, is natural, culture is a natural thing. It is the substratum of two extremes: the acquittal of as many as have been predestinated unto this acquittal, or the banishment of those who have been foreordained to this banishment.

Grace is not inherent in culture (*colere*) as such. Nor is grace inherent in eating and drinking as such, or in breathing, or in the begetting of children. Grace, if there is grace, would be inherent only in God-fearing *colere*, eating and drinking, and begetting of children — not as dead but as living people.

And the curse does not lie in culture (*colere*) as such. Nor does it lie in eating and drinking as such, or in breathing, or in the begetting of childen. The curse, if there is a curse, would lie only in ungodly *colere*, ungodly eating, drinking, and begetting of children — not as living but as dead people.

Within the framework of time after the Fall, the antithesis was inevitable not in nature but in the use of nature, and hence in culture. This is the antithesis between cultural activity in faith and in unbelief.

There is indeed "common" grace in culture (grace for more than one person). But there is no universal (or general) grace for all men. Therefore Abraham Kuyper's construction was wrong.

There is indeed also a "common" curse in cultural life (a curse shared by more than one person). But there is no universal (or general) curse.

"Common" can sometimes be the same as universal, but it is not necessarily always so. Something can be common to all people, but it can also be common to more than one person, not to all.

In the present scheme "common" is intended to mean: shared by many, not by all people.

There is a common (not: universal) grace in culture, as far as the redeeming work of Christ is shared by all those who are His — which grace has an effect upon their cultural achievements. But all the others lie under the common curse. It has been given to the Man of Acts 17:31[10] to pronounce judgment over them.

**19.** Immediately after the Fall the Son of God took action, not yet as Jesus but as the Messiah, known to God alone, being the *Logos asarkos incarnandus*, the Word not yet incarnate which yet had to come into the flesh. He took action in order to begin the work and the ministry of grace in this world, and to mark as being determined by *His* work the ground (not of election and reprobation, for their ground is only God's good pleasure, but) of salvation and of condemnation. The ground of salvation would be: Christ's merits. The ground of condemnation would be: man's guilt, which after the Fall appeared to be determined by the presence of Christ's work. Man's guilt is his rejection of Christ. Thus Christ took action as the Saviour-Redeemer, and as the Saviour-Avenger. The constitutive element in both functions is: His evangelical work of redemption, which is never satisfied with being a negligible quantity.

Because in this spirit and with this double intention, Christ, before the countenance of God, took upon Himself the burden of the world, He became the Redeemer of the world, culture included. He also gave — from now on Christologically determined — meaning to all cultural activity. This Christologically determined sense is universal, general. The grace therein is not universal, but common. It is the one and only grace unto salvation, redemptive and re-creating grace. For Christ now guarantees that the world, which in God's eternal counsel was "foreordained," will return to God, its Creator.

Accordingly a complete history of many centuries is for His sake "inserted" between the first sin ever committed and the final curse. We repeat: for His sake. After what we have said, this cannot mean: only for the sake of His redemption work (or only for the sake of the elect). It must mean: for the sake of His double function as the Saviour-Redeemer and the Saviour-Judge. He makes room for history in order that all that happens may be Christologically determined: pro as well as con. And of course the verb "insert" is no more than metaphorical language. History only *seems* to be "inserted." But in reality it was determined from eternity. In history God makes room for Christ's all-dominating work of redemption, and for His appearing, presently as Jesus, in order to die here on earth, rise again from the dead, and change the course of the world by shifting its helm with hands of flesh and blood through the power of God's Spirit.

In this history even of a fallen world, a history created by God's will so that this world might hold its own, Christ must be considered as the One Who carries all the burdens of the world, while He transfers all the world's delights to God the Father, that God may be all in all — see the concluding verses of I Corinthians 15. So God directs all that happens in this world towards Christ. He directs all cultures towards Christ, Who shall determine the fulness of time; the culture of the ancient nations before the Flood, that of Egypt, Persia, Rome, Greece, and Babylon. Such prophets of Christ's advent as Isaiah and Daniel are the instructors of every true cultural philosopher. Because of Him and also by Him every process is led to this *pleroma* of time. And therefore every culture has to serve in order to make room for a seemingly a-cultural manger, and for an also seemingly culturally indifferent cross, and in order to have a hole hewn out presently, somewhere in a garden belonging to Joseph of Arimathea. But on the Easter morning the body of this Son of Man then rises again from this grave, being whole and sound and flawless. Then He returns to God's world in the Spirit, this Christ Jesus, and puts the world in its own place. He puts sound — that is to say: reborn — people in the place that is fitting for them and He heals life, in so far as life acknowledges Him as the mystical (i.e., hidden) Head of His community.[11]

Hereby the respective relations are brought back, in principle, to their ethically normal origin (as we have seen, the original norms are the natural ordinances for created life). Flesh and blood do not proclaim any ethical norms, but only the Spirit, through God's Word — even concerning the governing, stimulating, and eschatological subservience of flesh and blood.

Hence, when the world was top-heavy with an effete and violently disruptive pseudo-culture which did not acknowledge God as the Owner of the cosmos, a handful of simple gild artisans in some small towns in Asia Minor — workers who by the preaching of the Gospel of Christ had learned to serve God in their daily labour — as often as they had dutifully, with God in mind, tanned a piece of leather or made a tent or completed a certain gild task, meant more, precisely for culture, than the entire imperial train of the Caesar of Rome with his palaces, his dancers, his laurels, his maecenasses, and his metropolis. Hence, when on a certain day an escort of prisoners was led into the city of Rome, among whom there was a certain Paul, this man was of greater significance, particularly for cultural life, than all of culture-drunk Rome: he signified a radical change, over against all those prominent ones who were running the show — he who called himself a "miscarriage."

Yes, indeed, this is true, says someone, for later on Paul would create culture through his followers. But no, say the angels, he created culture right then, at that very moment. A man who was sound, a man of God, entered into the wilted and corrupt city of Rome, a maker of tents and a philosopher, a theologian and missionary: someone who would have the courage to look the emperor in the eye. even when the latter did not have the courage any more to do the same to him. A man who showed his fellow prisoners a great light. and made a rented house in Rome the forecourt of an academy of philosophy. There is a little poem by a Latin poet that says: .

*Occurri nuper. visa est mihi digna relatu*
*pompa: senem potum pota trahebat anus.*

That is. in the street I met a strange procession: a drunken old hag was dragging a drunken old fellow. Pardon this crude translation, but it is fitting here. This little song in its realism as well its cultural-historical outspokenness is as typical of the days in which the apostle Paul entered the culture-drunk city of Rome as that other little song in which a Roman emperor pitied his "soul" because of its poverty, and, blasé, wished it goodnight. Yes, indeed, this was typical of the big city of those days: drunkenness, which is then considered to be a joke. The relationships were turned completely upside down: the woman drags the man behind her, grey hair is no longer an elegant crown, and the poet, chuckling over it, makes capital out of it. Here we see the downfall of that entire world. But then the apostle Paul entered the city. in chains, for the servant is not higher than his Master. However, this Paul — although he had a thorn in the flesh and, according to his own statement in I Corinthians 15:8. had been brought into the Church as a "miscarriage," and although he knew himself incorporated into the procession of the not many rich, the not many noble, the weak ones, and those who are nothing in this world, I Corinthians 1 — this man Paul was, by the grace given to him, an example of soundness, also of cultural soundness. In the same way the seven epistles, hidden somewhere in the beginning of an Apocalypse, the book of Revelation, are, by the grace that speaks in them, monuments of culture. Such is what they are as truly as the Sermon on the Mount is a monument not only of the history of revelation but also of cultural history. For in the Sermon on the Mount, Jesus Christ teaches us here on earth, and in these seven epistles the same Jesus Christ teaches from heaven, how at the trough, at the office, in the temple, in the factory, at the academy, and in the artist's studio, one has to realize again that one's startingpoint, purpose, and direction are determined by God, that he has to fill his "yes" and "no" with the strength of an oath, and to do his work under the tension of living between the beginning and the end of history as a *kohen*, i.e., as one who "stands and serves" before God. In the Sermon on the Mount and in those seven epistles the world turns the other way round, just as it had to do, in order to prepare a cradle and to set up a workshop, even if it were only for one single man of God. Herein Christ in principle condemns for everyone the fragmentation of life and conquers it in the life of His own people. He fundamentally connects the respective faculties until they have grown into a complete "university." He again links "religion" together with "culture," making cultural activity into a concrete service of God, and, when it comes to the point, denies anything that is not out of God the name and honour of "positive cultural activity." For, strictly speaking, all is sin that is not out of faith. The cultural urge *per se* is, as we have seen, one of the "natural" gifts, the "gifts of creation." Therefore we can also speak of *colere* in the animal kingdom. Who knows if there some progress is made in matters of organization? Who knows if even the ants and the bees have shown a certain "progress" in the building of their nests and in the way of gathering and preserving honey? But the purposeful use of these gifts of creation, positive cultural activity in accordance with the commandment given by God with respect to purpose and eschatologically determined direction, is possible only in an obedience regained through the Spirit of Christ. Sin, wherever it may appear, also in cultural life, is unable to be persistently moral in its cultural thinking, nor can it build or create in a culturally positive way. For *colere* means "to build," but sin breaks down. In God's original dictionary of revelation "culture" is always constructive, but sin is destructive. We shall come back to this point later on.

As it was in the days when Paul stumbled into the city of Rome, so has it always been in the world since then. Every reformation that, driven by the Spirit of Christ, returns to the Scriptures, the Word of God, is at the same time a healing of culture. When round-headed Martin Luther at last got married and could laugh again in a healthy way, he was worth a hundred ducats as a healing and direction-giving producer of culture, while the complete papal and imperial train was worth hardly more than one single ducate, even considered from the cultural point of view. This is evident when one compares the spheres of activity of Lutheran and Roman-Catholic countries. However, while Luther made certain errors in the foundation principles, or, let us put it this way, in the fundamentals of the relation between nature and grace — which errors were overcome by John Calvin — the Calvinistic countries later exhibited a cultural development that thetically and antithetically was far stronger and produced far greater strength than was the case in Lutheran countries. The cultural chaos that Adolf Hitler left behind because he first brought it with him, could arise in Lutheran countries also with the support of "orthodox" Lutherans, but met positive and unbreakable resistance among the Calvinistic groups. This resistance

51

did not weigh off "values" which can be directly grasped and which possess a tangible usefulness against other "values" ("Americanism," communism versus Nazism, real democracy versus a mythical *gesundes Volksempfinden!*), but it continuously kept in mind the far-reaching protological and eschatological history projects of the Apocalypse, which encompass all of history, and consequently connected its cultural activities with the fundamental principles of the Calvinistic Reformation. John Calvin in Geneva and Strasbourg shows us what the service of God is concretely able to do also for cultural life. He created a Christian culture, which had been freed from the secularist-imperialist aspirations that still render Rome's imagination effete since they are inspired by the same false distinction between "nature" and "grace" that played Martin Luther a trick.

As often as we think about these things it strikes us that the name which the book of Revelation applies to the Roman Empire and which is so meaningful precisely for cultural evaluation and examination, is that of the anti-christian prototype, the name "harlot." When the Bible calls the Roman Empire a harlot, all depends on the right exegesis. The same is true when Martin Luther gives the philosophical *Seminare* a hard nut to crack when speaking about *die Hure Vernunft* (the harlot Reason). This was no condemnation of "reason" (for a harlot does not stand condemned because of her womanly nature) but of the proud and sinful reason which has emancipated itself from God (just as in a harlot only the use of her womanly nature contrary to the divine ordinance for womanhood is to be accursed). One single false interpretation of the word "harlot" that does no longer distinguish between the one thing and the other, is all that is needed to throw Martin Luther — wrongly, of course — on the despised heap of the despisers of God's great gift of reason. In the same way, one indiscriminate interpretation of the term "harlot" in the Apocalypse, and the Church of Rome no longer knows in what particular respect the Roman Empire was a harlot. Was it a harlot in its persecution of Christians? O no, that was only the consequence. It was a harlot when it refused to put the created gifts at the disposal of God, Who wants to be the Bridegroom of His faithful work-community. Then, as a consequence of such a false exegesis, a world-wide Church can become enamoured of what ultimately is the harlotry of the Roman Empire. Then a church presents itself that acts as "the state," idealizing the state as a cultural *power*, and imitating it even at the cost of mutilating the prophetic cultural *testimony*, and this way forgetting that the *prophecy* concerning the relation between nature and grace (and also between nature and sin) which is faithful to God's Word is a greater cultural force than the most astonishing Pyrrhic victory of a culturally expansive church. Over against such a Pyrrhic victory of Rome, John Calvin meant a restoration. He built up a Christian, Protestant, Reformed culture, precisely by making a distinction — which does not mean a separation — between church and state. He came to God's recruits with an order-of-the-day that was also a matter of culture. He saw again that in the Old Testament the "shepherds" had a wider task than only that of caring for souls, for they were commissioned with cultural care as well. He again taught a living love for the divine calling, went out into all the nooks and crannies of the world, and had learned to understand that precious word of grace and hence also of culture: "All things are yours . . . and ye are Christ's; and Christ is God's" (I Corinthians 3:21, 23).

And this is the law that shall remain in force in this world.

A church magazine that, wherever necessary, does its weeding and keeps principles pure means more for culture than a gilded stage. Over against a minister who in a "Reformed weekly" exclaimed that sometimes one single drama means more than seven study outlines, the Reformed distinction of nature-grace-sin maintains that one good outline means more than seven, even good, dramas, in as much as the power of God's Word is stronger than that of the image, and doctrine is more than sign. A Christian family, living in a distinctively Christian style, is for cultural life, in whatever complications it may be placed, another revelation of the wholesome power for which one looks in vain in Hollywood, of which a culturally sorry portrayal — sorry especially from a cultural point of view — is given in Vicky Baum's book, *Leben ohne Geheimnis*. A Christian labourer who dares to be himself as Christian, again represents wholesomeness in an unhistorical, businesslike-Americanized world; he is worth more in potential force than a complete college of science that has not seen God.

Thus Christ continuously works in all His people until the end of time. In this world, which has to complete its course according to His operative Easter rights, He time and again brings to the fore new forces for cultural life in its widest sense, performing in the republic of the communion of saints a *creative* miracle: for *every regeneration*, acknowledged in Calvinistic fashion as a new *creation*, is a matter of His transcendent and merciful intervention in cultural life also. He continues and He will presently open new fountains as often as in the life of an individual, or subsequently in a community, efforts are undertaken and work is done in His power and in accordance with His revealed Word.

Therefore the book of Revelation draws a picture of the pure cultural-city-at-rest of the future, the new Jerusalem, with its perfect style, a style truly satisfying its inhabitants. No, this new cultural city — new because of its having come into existence by renewal and its being elevated above the level of struggle — does not come into being gradually.

The "catastrophe" of the last day is essential for its appearance — just as "catastrophes" played a prominent role in the creation.[12] However, let us not forget that at the moment when this catastrophe takes place, whether "in heaven above" or "in the earth beneath" or "in the water under the earth," all spiritual and material potentials are already present that are necessary to build or restore this cultural city and, then, according to His commandment, continuously to fashion the material made available by God's providence to His community of men, to fashion it in a "logical" way — which means here, through the Logos Who became flesh and has declared God to us. This catastrophe itself will not create chaos, nor destroy or trample upon any seed. On the contrary, it will purge and purify this cosmos of every culture-destroying element or "producer" of cultural disintegration. For when God opens the new heaven, then this new heaven will not be, so to speak, a *donum super-additum* that has been obtained by a new act of creation and has done away with the old creation or covers and encloses it. This new Jerusalem will overshadow the old dwelling-place of man but not cover it like a dome. The never-ending story of the wonder of this dwelling-place of God among men will not be mechanically added and imposed as a completely new chapter that is to follow the narrative of the history of our world as a sort of appendix, but it shall only be an undiluted and unrestrained Gospel report concerning the unhindered development — given by God in Christ — of all those forces that were put by Christ in the new (that is, renewed) mankind, the community of the servants of God, and were already initially developed therein.

20. Here we briefly have to return to a point that has been touched on in the above. We said there that, strictly speaking, the granting of a licence for positive cultural activity can occur only when people build and labour *according to God's will*.

This may be too strong a statement, in many people's opinion.

We immediately admit that it needs some further amplification, even though we have already referred to the fact that the act of *colere* is natural to all people, in so far as they as a result of their innate urge to work and move participate in the cultivation and development of the cosmos according to their being involved as creatures in the never idle field of the world.

Yet there is a possibility of misunderstanding which must be avoided.

For after the Fall God did not split up the world into two halves, one of which would perform cultural service according to God's commandment, the other being a desert or a chaos containing only ruins and caricatures. The mere thought is already foolish. This idea does not only clash with the obvious facts but it also trifles with every presupposition of cultural activity.

No real koinōnia exists among men unless it has been brought about by God's Spirit. Koinōnia means communion. It does not owe its existence to the simple fact that various people have the same nature or the same interests. For if this in itself would establish a community, then there would be a covenant communion everywhere. Then there could not be a hell. Those who are of the opinion that communion is already established by the sharing of the same nature and interests, forget that the same thing is essential also for quarrelling and fighting with one another in such a way that the one really touches the other. No, real communion is something else. It can only be achieved wherever the same nature is directed towards a common goal through love for the same basic principles and wherever the same interests are promoted in common faith and hope and love. Cultural koinōnia, then, is basically a matter of the fellowship of faith. Here our remarks concerning the antithesis to be found also in cultural life are applicable.

However, while koinōnia joins only part of mankind together, there exists a sunousia, a being-together, among all men.

Now God has imposed sunousia upon all men. Wheat and chaff have not been finally separated from one another. One day even this sunousia will be taken away from them. However, things have not yet reached that point. Towards all those people placed next to each other in sunousia comes the command to engage in cultural labour (which mandate is general because God has not abolished any command that is original and permanent in character) just as also the urge to cultural labour is an inborn one.

Besides, the given material to be fashioned is the world inhabited by us (and who can say if even the world not yet inhabited by us will not become part of our area of endeavour?). For that reason there cannot be the cultural performance of the one without that of the other. The koinōnia is given us by Christ, the sunousia comes from God the Creator.

There is only one nature, but a twofold use of nature; one material, but a twofold fashioning of it; one territory, but a twofold development of it; one cultural urge, but a twofold cultural striving.

And since all fashioning of the material, the good as well as the bad, is bound to the nature, the structure, and the laws of that particular material, the products of the labour of the unbeliever and those of the labour of the believer are very much alike. This similarity is not caused by the similarity of their diverging minds but by that of the stiff, recalcitrant material. There is a great difference between the one potter and the other, between the one sculptor and the other. The one builds a temple, the other builds a dancing hall, but both of them go for their clay to the same pit and for their marble to the same quarry.

This is the first aspect.

There is also a second one.

We touch here the problem of the "common tempering." For God has arrested the course of human sin. Now the stiffness of the material to be fashioned still remains and shall remain to the last day. But also the will to free oneself from the material — Fichte in his philosophy at least dreamt of such "freedom" — is checked in its advance of satanic pride in this world of general tempering. Christ (for this checking or arresting is an act of God's providence and, consequently, determined by the history of revelation and salvation) has bound Satan so that he can no longer devour the nations during the period of time indicated in Revelation 20, except in the last period of the "thousand years" that comprise the progress from Ascension Day and Pentecost until the Parousia. He has tempered the process of sin and curse; the "withholding" of Antichrist is a matter of fact. However, this withholding of Antichrist corresponds with the holding-Himself-in of Christ Triumphant. He, too, does not let Himself go. He, too, does not yet allow this world, which is still tempered and held in check in all its life's movements, the view of the full expansion of His exalted power. All the carts are still held in check, all the horses are bridled. Judgment is held back, but so is grace, in *this* world.

Therefore nothing is fully developed and consummated, nothing is mature as yet. Nowhere has the power of Christ's mercy revealed itself in its full strength, not even in heaven. Neither has Satan's destructive power, according to his own scheme, made its influence felt in full strength anywhere in the world, not even in hell. Any kind of music, of angels as well as of demons, is *wohltemperiert*, and the One Who controls it is God.

This is the mystery of the common tempering in the problem of culture (the substratum of the above-mentioned common grace and common judgment). Life has not yet split up into the forms of hell and heaven. The godless are still prevented in their cultural labour from ecstatically raging against God in the paroxysm of satanism, although this is in a direct line with their hidden desire; and the communion of God's saints, partly by the sin that dwells in them but also by the governing of their king Himself, Who is pursuing the goals of the history of salvation and revelation, is still prevented from doing adequately what is their line. Thus by the rule of Christ, who restrains everything until the last day, there is, for those who serve God as well as for those who do not serve Him, the possibility of being simultaneously engaged in work on one and the same cultural fragment, now here, then there — work that takes place in *sunousia* and is bound by the structure of the material of the cosmos.[13] Those who serve God and those who do not serve Him have not been geographically separated in the world. Christ Himself keeps them still together. In this mixed and restrained world it is still possible to do constructive work even though the constructors are not men of God. No ark was ever built by only Noah's family. The candidates for death are always contributing their part.

However, we must also observe a third aspect; namely, that *temperantia* is always constant, but the *restraint* or tempering is not. Until now we have mentioned these two in the same breath. That was permissible, for God tempers (i.e., controls, guides, keeps in check) by means of restraint (by withholding). But *temperantia* is a matter of *governing* (something which remains for ever, also in heaven and hell, and in all ages), and restraint is a special *manner* of governing (which manner may change). Revelation, chapter 20, and also II Thessalonians, chapter 2, tell us that Satan will be loosed, which will happen *within* the duration of time, and that the "withholder" of Antichrist one day (also within time) will "be taken out of the way." This restraint will never completely be lacking in this world. For completely absent it will be in heaven and in hell. However, within the duration of time it will not be of a constant measure. The one day it is stronger that the other. In certain periods, God hands the people over to their delusive ideas, and sends (!) them an "energy" of error (with horrible cultural effects), and in other periods He awakens in His Church the Spirit of repentance and conversion, Who sometimes causes the impact of the preaching of God's Word to penetrate very deeply even into the circles of the unbelievers. This restraint, then, will decrease to a minimum at the end of time. Then any *status quo* existing between the Church and the world will be denounced — from both sides — also in cultural life, even precisely there. Then the whole world — except God's elect — will crowd together around the Antichrist. Then his (cultural) miracles — which God allows him to perform by His active permission, that is, by making cosmic material (with its inherent possibilities, as discovered with astonishing speed) freely accessible — will, as so many signs and wonders of falsehood, brush aside the Church with its proclamation of the truth and push it into the distant corner of antiques and of separatist, rectilinear-minded fanatics. Then the flames of the cultural struggle will flare up as never before: the propaganda of falsehood will appear to be "supported" by some dazzling facts, while the propagation of the truth will be solely dependent on the faithful Word that under those circumstances shows its confessors the meaning of the "hard" saying: "Blessed are they that *have not seen, and yet have believed*" (John 20:29).

We are living in an interim to be so understood, in the interim-of-the-interim.

We have already discussed the former: the interim between the first and the last things of ("ordinary") history.

The latter has been indicated in the above: it is the interim between the not yet anti-christian era and the presently indeed anti-christian parousia of the one man of sin, the great cultural hero, though hero in sin, escorted by the propaganda department of the false prophet: the beast from the earth (Revelation, chapter 13).

May the knowledge thereof make the believers careful as never before. Even when the cultural forms are the same, he should distinguish the differences in cultural *direction*.

For when under the impact of the law of tempering and the restraint by God there is "still" a possibility of a wide scope of development of science and art, of trade and industry, of national and international communication, of technology or whatever else, then this is indeed "still" "culture" to a certain degree. But this "still" is determined by the fact that Satan has "not yet" been loosed. Who does not feel the drift towards the end of the interim-of-the-interim when he has neard Bach and . . . jazz? In so far as cultural activities are not driven by faith, not done according to the Law of God and to His honour, they operate with corrupt "remnants," and are in fact a mere residue. The material (of Genesis 1, cosmic nature) has remained. And there are still remnants, residues, of the original gifts.

The word "residues" is, of course, not meant only in a quantitative sense, for although there are still some quantitatively measurable "remnants" of the original gifts left, the quantitative can shrivel up and will indeed do so. Therefore these remnants are also called *vestigia*, or vestiges, i.e., footprints. "*Vestigia*" is not a quantitative concept, for the footprints left by a dog's paw or a man's shoe are not remnants thereof. Acknowledging the double fact that there will always be remnants of the original gifts — the tempering is constant — but that they will become smaller and smaller and the "light of nature" more and more suppressed (Canons of Dort), and that (for the believer, according to the strength of his faith's understanding) there will always be clear *vestigia* in this drunken world, vestiges of the paradisal gifts (even in anti-christian cultural infatuation), we nevertheless speak, in this sense and with these reservations, of remnants and *vestigia*. Our conclusion then is that culture is never more than a mere attempt and that, since it is restricted to remnants only, it is a matter of tragedy. God has indeed left something behind in fallen man. But these are only "small remnants" of man's original gifts, concerning which the Calvinistic confession speaks in such a brilliant-dangerous way.[14] Even when they have been reduced to their minimum or defiled to their maximum (Canons of Dort), they are still vestiges. In the imminent pandemonium of the cultural revolution against God and His Anointed, the believer shall discover the *vestigia* of the riches of paradisal life — but he alone. The anti-christian cohorts shall not see therein the vestiges of "yesterday," but only the *primitiae*, the firstlings of "tomorrow," for which tomorrow they hope (in vain), and which is cut off by the heavenly Judge. Until then we Christians shall continue to build, in hope against hope — just as Noah built the ark, in his "last days." We know it: these remnants, taking effect in a world that is "withheld" by God according to the measure of all His times and wherein not a single vulcano of sin, not a single hearth of grace, can empty itself in an absolute ,and adequate way, a world that day after day is preserved against the *summum* of its own destruction, and is continuously protected against the unlimited success of its own destructive tendencies — these residues of such a world are still able, according to the scheme of development and restraint that Christ's Sender maintains in the Christological progress of all history, to instigate new cultural contributions, as long as it pleases Him. This is an instigation the possibility of which was already given in the paradisal world, and which has its *kairos* only because Christ has His own aim and intention with the world and has reserved it unto the fires of judgment day. However, the residues in question can never force a breakthrough, or, what is even worse, they can never produce any work that is sound, accurately directed to meet its objective, and true to its style, not even work that is true to nature. For bound to nature is entirely different from true to nature. In one's acting (in a responsible way and intervening in history) one is only true to nature when one is ethically faithful to its Maker. A culture that wants to maintain itself apart from God cannot reach consummation if it constantly continues to follow the course it has chosen. It never can come to unity. It will never mature. All through the centuries it consumes and scatters itself. The unregenerate detains what he retains (he holds it in unrighteousness, Romans 1:18; Canons of Dort III/IV, Article 4). A single continuing style has never been born wherever Christ was not acknowledged as the Legislator. Time and again the monster of imminent cultural paralysis appears alongside the cultural tendencies that have made themselves felt in nations, races, and societies: the architects may be building, but the original design has been lost. They are building fragmentarily. Every century has its own *fin-de-siècle*. All that which is heavy becomes top-heavy. With the help of cultural instruments — take, e.g., the cinema, which was the result of cultural building but which, once it was there, should have been a cultural instrument and then could have kept its place in the pedagogic whole — people are not going to build but to destroy: they will rob God. Every builder will become bankrupt as soon as his employees fall in love with their tools, refine and "cultivate" them for their own sake but in the meantime show no love for the activity of building. Those who remember this know: our Chief Builder (God) will never go bankrupt, but yet He has a multitude of that contemptible sort of bricklayers and labourers, also among His Christian people. For even among them there are fools who concerning any cultural instrument cry out: the cultivation of it is real culture! They feel ashamed not to join in with others. But this is foolishness. The cultivation of a cultural instrument in itself and for its own sake is nothing but idolatry — it falls under the same heading as the worship of idols, which also includes the personalism that we rejected earlier. A film for the sake of the film, sports for the sake of sports, fine arts for the sake of fine arts, all have had something to do with culture; but the technique of cultivating these so-called "territories" (oh dear!), apart from the goal and from the whole of the one universal territory of operation of the world that must be brought back to God, is as an activity not a matter of building but of breaking down: *agape* for the cultural goal then yields to *eros* with respect to the cultural means. With the help of a hammer one can build but also destroy. So this world is destroyed not by sports, the cinema, etc., but by their being isolated as goods-in-themselves. The movies in our days are being technically perfected more and more. However, the cinema is not a constructive but a destructive thing. Instead of being a medium of education it has become a means of blinding the people's eyes. Whoever calls this activity culture because the cinema originates in cultural power, forgets that *colere* still means "to build or cultivate," not "to break down." Even Satan can only fight against us with the help of the material that is available to him in the world of our *sunousia*. Concerning the Antichrist the same thing can be said. The beast of Revelation 13 does not enter into our world as through a funnel but has been with us in our *sunousia* from our very birth.

21. It is true that in the last days, when God abolishes the interim-law of His restraint and in an acute dramatic tension will rapidly bring upon the world the catastrophe of the great judgment, the Antichrist will set up a plan of action in order quickly to put over against any aspect of culture that is still slightly reminiscent of Christian influence an anti-culture of sin before the eyes of the world, and that he will try to complete an anti-programme. But in order that we may be able to understand what this means for our subject, we have to pay attention to two things: *First*, the Antichrist is a dictator. *Second*, he will be thrown from the battlements, on which he is glorifying himself, "half-way through his days."

In the first place he is, as we said, a dictator. This means that the origins of his activities, also of his demonic anti-culture plans, do not proceed along the normal ways of development from what already exists, but are by force thrust upon a world that is divided against itself. According to the strict rules of the logic of God's judgment of hardening the hearts as it is passed on the world, God Himself will enable him thereto. The "democratic" world shall undergo its punishment when it ends up with the Gilt Dictator. How and whereby will God enable him to do this evil work? By His above-mentioned "active permission," which grants to the Antichrist the making of as many discoveries as are needed for the "miracles of Antichrist" (II Thessalonians 2, Revelation 13). He will show off with them: the materials of the cosmos will presently be used in the grandiose game of the ultimate, organized immorality. The infatuation with cultural fragments, cultural flashes, and cultural instruments — barely registered, because they were miraculously invented — will then push its way through and develop into the most frivolous exhibitionism, a carnival of immorality, unashamed and respecting neither God nor man. "*Colere*" will come to an end, the setting of long-term goals will cease, and, because of the mere infatuation with cultural *things*, the cultural *commission* as God gave it will be rejected. But we must add: this hard reality will not be acknowledged unless among the greatly reduced number of the last, persecuted Christians. This infatuation with cultural *things* will identify as the cultural *mandate* the praise of man for man. Those who do not join in the singing of this praise will be sentenced as spoilsports: dictators know no mercy.

And the fact which we mentioned in the second place, that in

God's judgment the Antichrist will be thrown from the high battlements "halfway through his days," proves that the development of his own style can not be finished and his programme not completed. Any culture of infatuation excludes real love and must disappear as smoke is driven away, for it is the final convulsive twitch of "the wicked" of Psalm 68. This will mean punishment for the Antichrist, his judgment. Yes, indeed. But it will at the same time mean the revelation of his impotence: every judgment corresponds with the immanent condition of the person concerned.

Therefore it is so appropriate that the last book of the Bible tells us that the figure 7 fits the work of *God*, as also the number 1000, the number of perfect completion, but that the Antichrist can get no further than the figure $3\frac{1}{2}$. That is to say, halfway (for $3\frac{1}{2}$ is half of 7) his work will be broken, together with himself. The "culture" of the Antichrist will presently leave in its wake only torsos, when the horizon bursts aflame with the fire that will be seen even at the shore of the sea of glass, the fire of God's judgment. The anti-christian cultural fun-fair of the Serious Game, in honour of *Homo Ludens*, that idol, shall be the last spasmodic effort of man, who was created with the natural ability of a schematic mind, schematically (that is, in satanic and even satanistic style) to put over against God's *coetus* an anti-congregation. But the Bible, by writing the number $3\frac{1}{2}$ upon the glossy cultural products of this final "cultural struggle" and convulsion of sin, shows that the cultural structure of the last days is only a truncated pyramid.

Hereby shall be confirmed for the eye of faith what we have already stated; namely, that no one is able to build ecumenically, to *colere* homogeneously and continuously in the actual eschatologically determined sense of the word, unless he lives and works "from" God. Neither can any kind of community.

22. Over against the dismal picture of such a truncated pyramid stands the initially true-to-norm structure of the Church and the Kingdom of heaven, as far as the Word of God rules and prevails there.

This Kingdom prepared itself for the pain to be endured at the sight of this truncated pyramid. As often as the people of Israel or their kings forgot that the nation was also Church and that the Church in every struggle, including the cultural one, can only conquer through faith — that is, by joyfully accepting the contents of the revelation with which it has been entrusted — this nation alone with its royal house stood in tears at the sight of the stump of a once stately tree. David's house, Israel's national building, became such a stump. It became such particularly in cultural respect: the Babylonian exile. Jerusalem's destruction. Then the people, who had looked up to the culture of the "civilized nations" (the heathen), who had been eager to "compete" with them and to outbid them in the market of culture, said: Alas, no rod shall come forth out of the stem of Jesse! Who has ever seen anything so impossible? But then the prophets said: "Refrain thy voice from weeping, and thine eyes from tears" (Jeremiah 31:16). And Ezekiel had to become a sign unto the people who saw the destruction of the desire of their eyes — the desire of eyes that see cultural quantities only. He himself also lost the desire of his eyes (his wife) but was not allowed to mourn (Ezekiel 24:16, 25). Why not? Because for the faithful covenant congregation, which would take the Word of the covenant seriously again (Jeremiah 31), a rod would presently sprout forth out of the truncated stem, a "Branch," which would be the Christ, the Good Shepherd. He is a Shepherd because He provides in every need, also in cultural needs: Thy bread and thy waters shall be sure (Isaiah 33:16).

There we have the cultural activity of the faithful Church members: it is according to God's *promise*. This promise is of a cultural nature also; it has been given through grace and through the Gospel. This gift-of-grace will be "sufficient": "My grace is sufficient for thee" (II Corinthians 12:9). Sufficient to what end? Sufficient to reach the end of time in faithfulness to one's office and not to lose sight of *colere* or of the God Who always wants to be worshipped by His creatures.

We just said: it is sufficient. Is it not cultural pride to say that grace is sufficient? This is what "Neo-Calvinism" is reproached with.

No, we do not encourage any Christian cultural pride. For we said no more than that *grace* is sufficient. Besides, we acknowledged that also the Church and the Kingdom of God are living under the universal pressure of the law of restraint, this Sharp Resolution of Mitigation issued by Christ the King. Even the believers never finish their cultural endeavours. They, too, have their truncated pyramids. There is much patchwork in what they are doing. No, this is no reason for pride. For as a matter of fact the numbers 7 and 1000 fit God's Kingdom and Church not because they involve or include human labour but only because in both numbers Christ is effectively active with His Spirit. But — by this Christ has this great reality at least been proved: that sound and purposeful structure, norm-fast style, harmonious culture are present, truly present, only there where God by special grace again creates living people from the dead and where "men of God" are "furnished unto all good works" (II Timothy 3:17); there, moreover, wherever He mutually binds them and their works together. For teleologically-directed cultural construction is not an affair of individuals but of a strong communion. Therefore the article of our faith concerning "the communion of saints" (the *koinōnia*) is also of direct significance for culture. And a schism in the Church — a true schism, not what hierarchy makes of it — always means cultural destruction. On the other hand, Church reformation, even though the number of confessors may dwindle, is always cultural restoration also. And when those true confessors are boycotted and with violence removed from the workshops and funds of culture, they will still be evangelists, signposts of culture, even though they have been thrown aside. For the only one who may truly be called a source of culture is Jesus Christ.

We realize that this standpoint has been called "impertinent." However, those who made such statements do not share our "creed." They do not know a Word of God that effectually enters into history in a historical way; that is, continuously producing fruits from its own seed. The "Word of God" as they consider it is no "seed of regeneration." In their view, no "chain of salvation" is forged here, under the clouds of heaven. What produces fruits, thirty-, sixty-, and even hundredfold, here below, can in their opinion never have been seed from above.

We shall not further deal with this theory. We would be able seriously to oppose Barthianism only if we had been given more space than is available here.

However, let no one delude himself with the idea that this would be a clash of arguments only. For at bottom we have to make here a decision of faith. Either one acknowledges the Scriptures as the Word of God, or one does not acknowledge them as such. We very well realize that, as soon as we are deprived of the Scriptures, our standpoint cannot produce any proof for its being correct — just as the other standpoint cannot do so. But we do not want to make anything but a statement of faith, also this time. Not only matters concerning the Church and the forgiveness of sins are matters of faith, but of all things it must be said that they are only known through faith and not by "experience." Even questions regarding the "substance" and "appearance" of culture are answered by faith only. Concepts such as a "communion" and "to build" are matters of faith: if the confession had nothing to say concerning them, it would not deserve its name.

But because we accept this standpoint as the Biblical one, we do not shrink from its consequences.

Let us mention a few of them.

**23.** The *first* one is that, strictly speaking, it is incorrect to speak of "the" culture, of culture as such. This way of speaking uses an imaginary quantity; that is to say, in so far as it might suggest that there is unity of cultural endeavour. This unity is lacking even "transcendentally." Just as there is no *"reine"* Vernunft ("pure" reason), no *reine* Verstand *überhaupt* (pure intellect in general), there is no such thing as *reine Kultur* (pure culture). Although nature is one, there is more than one use and cultivation of nature. To will is inherent in man, also culturally; it belongs to his nature. But cultural striving is more than to will: it includes long-term and long-distance objectives.

Having arrived at this point, we again meet with the antithesis and with the curse that is the result of sin, the curse of disintegration and scattering. The world still dreams of a tower of Babel, and still its language is confounded wherever this great project is undertaken. It no longer occurs in the same striking way as at the first Tower of Babel. It happens more gradually now. The punishment is never so severe nor the curse so immense as when things go this gradual way. In principle there is again some *einheitlich* (unified) cultural producing, born from the Spirit of God. But because the unbeliever, that great sectarian, turns away from it — while nevertheless at the approaches to the cultural material to be fashioned he more and more posts his sentries, who turn back everyone that is unable or unwilling to produce the password of sin (presently this will be the name of the beast) — therefore the culture that is built through faith will cover smaller and smaller areas. This culture is *einheitlich*, but of the material that affords "opportunities" for the cultural impulse it uses no more than fragments only. The world of unbelieving schismatics — sin is schismatic — does not want it any other way. Over against this stands the fact that this schismatic "world" itself, even though it conquers all the approaches towards the natural sources, the material to be fashioned and cultivated and the already discovered cultural means, because of its sinful character and the inherent destruction of communion, produces no more than mere cultural fragments in its presently almost universal cultural territory. With the believers there is unity in labour but only fragmentation of work areas. With the unbelievers there is a unified work area but fragmentation of the work: fragments, torsos, exponents of the diverging aspirations and endeavours which are not out of God, contradict each other, cancel each other out, and are never able to consolidate themselves into a unity. For the imposed unity of the totalitarian anti-christian state will not last long: if it were not imposed, this sham unity would fall to pieces.

We have already seen it, partly with a feeling of shame: even culture that is in accordance with the will of God shall not reach completion before judgment day. As far as this is a matter of the universal law of the already discussed retardation of powers; the "restraint," it makes us humble: our life is but short and we are dependent on the "climate" in which we are born. As far as this is a matter of being plundered by "the world" that ousts us from the "territory" still to be cultivated, we have to carry Christ's cross. As far as it is a matter of the sin of us all, which (we now follow the infralapsarian line) has from alpha to omega disturbed the gradual development of the first-given (cultural) world, and now makes unavoidable the sharply rising and falling line in the curve of the retardation of beast and Spirit, we have to profess our sin in Adam before God. And as far as the fact that we cannot finish our task is more a matter of our directly individual sin and of our slothfulness and unwisdom, we have to do penance for that and the more exert ourselves in working towards a sound, rich, and broad cultural life as long as this is still possible. For Christ puts before us *the duty of cultural activity*. Not to join in cultural labour means wilful disobedience on the part of God's labourers. It means not to serve God *in what belongs to Him*.

But we also have to distinguish God's governing hand in the fact that "culture as such," that of the believers no less than that of the unbelievers, cannot be finished, for God does not let any power fully develop itself, not even the power of Christ and His Spirit, before the great catastrophe of the last judgment. Retardation, we said, is the will of Christ, and the law set for the Antichrist, until the hour of Christ's parousia has come. Against a "law," a fixed ordinance, man's power can do nothing. We cannot so challenge the bull that he will enter the arena before the set time. We cannot avert God's restraining hand. Heavy as well as lightening, oppressive but with the unbreakable intention of God to grant us as yet "times of refreshing," it hangs over the world and its bustle, but let us not forget: this law works also in an evangelical way. It is of a Christological nature. God does not permit the thermometers of culture to be broken by premature heat, also for this reason: that He is waiting for the last one of the elect, as well as for the latter's opposite, the last reprobate. Both have yet to be born in this world. They will yet have to be surrounded by the earth's protecting atmosphere that grants them a place and without which no one can ever do any work. They must be immersed into the temperance-atmosphere that still tempers the hot glow of the heavy wrath of redemption, in order that at the very end of the lengthy course of time they may fulfil the counsel of God with regard to

66

themselves, contending with each other in a life-and-death struggle, the one armed, the other unarmed, each of them obeying a different command. Is there not in this retardation, in the atmosphere's not being rent apart, an awful kind of wrath, apart from astonishing grace? The retarding power lies upon world life as an atmospheric pressure. The balance will not be broken and the atmosphere not be rent before those last two will have completed their course. Then all those who are out of the second Adam will be allowed to take with them for ever the fruits of the cultural struggle as far as God's new world will make room for them. Then they will enter into the world of full satisfaction, which precisely as such does enjoy fruits of culture but has passed beyond all cultural striving. Then, but not before.

24. A *second* consequence of the standpoint we have taken is that in our discussion concerning the Christian and culture we must also not proceed from the fiction of "culture as such." There is not one single "cultural substance," certain "forms" of which we meet with or ourselves might "be." There is no universal soul or spirit or reason or logos. All these terms are mere abstractions. They would be more or less harmless if they were not always related to the pantheistic idea that the moral law accompanies universal culture itself because in culture "God" becomes "Self-conscious" and therein determines Himself. Over against this, the Christian professes that God does not come into existence but that He is there, that He has made His counsel from eternity and still makes it, and that He imposes His moral law *from above*. To *this* law we are bound in our actions. They are actions either of the new man that has been created by God or of the old man that has been dislocated by Satan. Therefore we are not trying to find a practical counterbalance in a Christian adaptation (supposing that such were possible) of a novel about *la peur de vivre*, over against the crypto-vitalistic designs of a "Christianized," touched up version of *Pallieter*, for example. We must serve God, everyone in his own way, wearing either a leather apron or an academic gown — it does not make any difference. Everyone has to serve God, wearing rubber boots or carrying a gasoline can, having as emblem a hammer and sickle (these belong to *us*) or a painter's palette, rather than a censer as such. We have to serve God, everyone in his own place in the new God-created community. "In his own place" means here: according to his own calling. For calling, not aspiration without inspiration, determines what is "ours." We have to detest thoroughly the forming of any group that fixes its limits and its criteria for membership while leaving the matter of divine calling beyond consideration. Everyone's individual character or disposition must be on

its guard against the danger of selfishly growing beyond its limits and must try to fit into the structure of the communion for which divine calling (to be known from the Scriptures and from the course of·our life) books us a place. To establish koinõnia in the sunousia, as members of the mystical union of Jesus Christ, that is Christian culture.

**25.** A *third* consequence of our standpoint regards the matter of *abstention* from cultural endeavour. Is there room for that? And if so, how far, why, and to what end?

This problem has many aspects, too many to sum up here. A few remarks may here suffice.

First of all, we must emphasize that, since there is a cultural mandate that existed even prior to sin, abstention from cultural labour is always sin: those who abstain from it are on strike. And now that Christ has comprised in Himself all the real treasures of "culture" — that is, of "grace" — abstention for the sake of abstention is nothing but a renunciation of Christ, self-imposed poverty, and sin before God. In this sense a Christian's abstention in cultural affairs should never be preached. "Every creature of God is good . . . if it be received with thanksgiving: for it is sanctified by the Word of God and prayer" (I Timothy 4:4, 5). It says: *every creature*.

The products of God's hands are not the same as ours: His "corn and wine" differ from our malt products or our distilled liquor. And precisely because every creature of God is sanctified by "the Word of God" (God's speaking to us) and by "prayer" (our speaking to Him), that is to say, in real covenant fellowship, abstention from cultural labour, or, in other words, the refusal to let God's creature appear in the covenant communion with God, is nothing but a matter of narrowing this communion. And what do we usually say about love that narrows its fellowship arbitrarily?

There is also a type of abstinence in which the faithful avoids certain areas of culture because he finds it too difficult to pursue God's command in those areas, deems himself incapable, considers the high pressure of being subject to God's Law too burdensome, and for this reason avoids that particular area. It should be clear that such abstinence is sinful. He avoids the cultural zone concerned because he does not want a conflict with God's Law. However, this abstinence is in reality an avoidance of God Himself. The person in question does not wish to get into trouble with Him, the Legislator, but at the same time he fails to let God show him His will. Renunciation of cultural participation may never be desired for its own sake. It can be justified and imperative only when it is imposed on us as an emergency measure.

For there will indeed be an emergency situation until the end of time. And this emergency situation will gradually grow even worse, for it is war-time.

Because of the war which God still wages against sin, and which sin wages against God, there is nowhere a possibility for a simultaneous, harmonious and centrally guided development of all cultural forces. Just as the normal development of the forces inherent in the life of a nation that is involved in a war is only possible as soon as the weapons are put down, so the community of the new mankind can find its "rest" only in normal labour on the new earth. Then the war will be over.

This war-motif shows us still another aspect of the matter of abstinence. God has millions of people in His creation, but only a part of those millions even begins to fulfil its duties. Therefore the communion of God's faithful children is much more heavily burdened than they ever would be if all people feared and served God. In our days frequent complaints are heard from the side of the unbelievers about the unequal distribution of goods. But those who complain about this apart from God are basically doing the very thing which they reproach society with. Go and take an evening walk past the movie theatres, have a look at the flashing signs and see how even the paupers in large numbers pay their two quarters. Think about the huge organization behind this powerless "cultural labour," which unfortunately is usually done in an unchristian way, and in this single example you will see proof of a God-less distribution of goods. The Christian labourer who toils to save a quarter and on Sunday puts it into the collection bag for mission work, is also engaged in "culture," be it indirectly. Half of this amount would have been enough for him to give if the idlers who spend their two quarters in the theatre had been able to find the dividing line between entertainment and labour, creative effort and recreation. The sums of money that are offered for one single bad film have been taken from, e.g., mission work, which is also cultural labour, although not exclusively. These few examples may illustrate the fact that Christians as a community are heavily burdened with respect to education, mission, Church life, charity, etc. At every step they are accompanied by abnormality, for the son who works in his Father's vineyard is overburdened because his brother who does not work is unfaithful to the Father.

Therefore, cultural abstinence, in whatever form and regarding whatever detail, as far as it originates in resentment, laziness, diffidence, slackness, or narrowmindedness, is sin before God. Unfortunately we must admit that in this regard the unbelieving world often rightly criticizes us. For quite apart from the resentment that

69

makes even Christians run down things they never can accomplish themselves, a quasi-edifying Pietism has all too often forgotten — and even branded as heresy — that the work of redemption leading us back to the "original" things imposes on the new man the duty of cultural labour. But on the other hand, in as far as the criticizing unbelievers, by neglecting their calling, are in fact on strike themselves and in cultural matters always decline a normal division of labour, Christians who consciously abstain are heroes when they resort to their negative "asceticism" to preserve the positive, their training for the forthcoming performance of their duties, putting first and foremost that whereto they are in particular called. A Christian people maintaining their colleges, supporting missionaries, and caring for the needy who were left them by Christ, thus saving them from the clutches of state-absolutism (that pioneer of the Antichrist!), doing a thousand other works of divine obligation, and primarily because of all this not able, for example, to set up an imposing Christian stage, supposing that such were possible, or to establish an extensive Christian organization of aesthetic and artistic character, such a people is indeed a heroic communion. When it voluntarily abstains for this reason, such abstention is, among other things, self-control and also self-denial, self-development of the man of God who wants to remain engaged in that whereto he has been called. Others may mock him, but he is herein dominated by a broad cultural insight. For his abstention because of the emergency situation places time under the arch of the history of the beginning as well as of the end. This sort of abstention should not be typified with the word "resentment," but finds its limits and legitimation in, e.g., Matthew 19:12, where Christ speaks about those "that make themselves eunuchs for the Kingdom of heaven's sake" and not in order to avoid this Kingdom. It recognizes itself in the scene presented in Revelation 12. There the woman (the Church) goes into the desert. Yet she — for she goes into the desert after Christ's ascension into heaven, at the beginning of the "thousand years" of His glorious reign — yet she has been liberated by the Son of man. She has the rights of Sarah, the free woman. But she suffers hunger in the desert together with Hagar, the bond woman. Her voluntary abstinence is definitely no negation of her hereditary rights, but the maintaining of her own style and a matter of taking in hand a cultural task which the majority of people never take into consideration: the service of God in the full extent of human life, *hic et nunc*, according to the occasion (*kairos*) of Christ's time (*chronos*).

It is war-time, even in our own heart. Also for this reason abstention may time and again be a duty for the individual person in very distinct respects that are individually to be more closely determined at every turn: hence the eye that is plucked out, the hand or the foot that is cut off, the field or the family that is left behind, the maimed body, the lonely soul, and all this for the sake of God's Kingdom. But this is again no abstention for the sake of abstention. It is a powerful effort to prevent an onerous distemperance from letting the lower lord it over the higher. In other words, it is not a matter of indifference to style, or hostility to culture, but, on the contrary, of culture-in-style, training and activation, self-temperance of the man of God in and unto service in the broadest sense.

**26.** A *fourth* consequence is that even within the framework of an inexact, non-scientific, popular parlance it is definitely incorrect to characterize the problem of "Christ and culture" as that of "common *grace*."

We have already expressed as our opinion that in an exact, conceptual description of our belief there is no room for the term "common grace," at least not in the Kuyperian sense, in which "common grace" is identified with "universal grace." We shall not elaborate further on this.

However, one could ask: Who is always prepared to produce an exact concept? Who is able to use a parlance that is fully adequate? Who is able to write one single page without using figurative language? In a certain definition, be it inexact but joyfully showing thanks for what is still left to us, could a cumulation of the vestiges of the creation gifts, and "natural light" and its use, not be called "grace"? Are we not permitted to take one single step together with the Remonstrants or Arminians, who (according to the Canons of Dort) designated "natural light" as "common grace"?

Our answer to this good-natured question is this time not so good-natured. This time we say no, and we believe that experience has taught a lesson here.

For in the first place there is some difference between "the glimmerings of natural light" that "remained" in man and the use of this light. The epic recitals in which Abraham Kuyper is presented as extolling common grace in the arts and sciences have more than once neglected the distinction between light and its use. But as soon as one raises the question what "grace" actually is, this distinction is of the greatest significance.

But apart from what we have said before, we have still another objection against the one-sided use of the word "grace." Nowadays we quite often hear people speak slightingly of "rectilinear" thought and of "single-track theology." Usually we then have some difficulty in keeping ourselves composed. It causes some extra difficulty when we hear this from certain authors who function as apologists of the Reformed Synods in The Netherlands in the years 1942-1944 (and even after 1946) and therefore march against those who really could not (to the exclusion of any differing view) hold the children of the covenant to be regenerated.[15] Sometimes we hear those apologists fulminate against the "rectilinear" and "single-track" thinking of their opponents. But they themselves had to promise (and with respect to *this* promise nothing changed) that they would not teach anything which was not in full agreement also with the synodical declaration of the year 1942 that took the trouble to assure us that "among us" (meant were those of Reformed confession) such residues in man as the "light of nature" were really called by the same name which also the Remonstrants used: common grace.

Well, this is too rectilinear to suit us. This reminds *us* of a single-track railway line. For "grace," being undeserved, forfeited "favour," is, then, a word related to the *idea of what is permissible.* Therefore many Christians have come to look upon the cultural problem as a question of what is and what is not permissible.

Hence the numerous accidents.

For in our opinion — and our whole argumentation confirms it — our cultural mandate must be primarily seen as a matter of a "common *command*," a "common *calling*," a "common *mandate*." Here our may is our must. Our above-explained standpoint shows the cultural question to be, even before the Fall, a question of duty, a mandate from the very beginning, a creature's service to God. And when the Heidelberg Catechism correctly and with full emphasis states that God does not wrong man when He requires of him that which had already been imposed on him in paradise, *even though he cannot do it any more*, then this answer turns its sharp edge against those who let their theory of "common *grace*" teach only and exclusively about that which by God's charter has been left to us as *being permissible. Dress the garden* — God does not wrong any man when He still requires the same thing of him, even though he cannot do it.

All this is closely connected with more than one important theorem, also of methodological structure. The doctrine of common grace that takes "grace" as its startingpoint, has chosen as the startingpoint for its problematic the things that after the Fall *have been left to us*. But here it makes more than one mistake. Without neglecting what happened after the Fall, it has to go back to what happened before the Fall in order to understand God's intentions. Further, time and again it speaks about that which has yet been left to *us*, us men, as if men were the more important here, rather than God. This theory is more anthropocentric than theological. And by making this mistake it necessarily makes a third one: it starts to broadcast culturally-optimistic sounds in a culpable way. For "nature" (as the material to be fashioned or developed by man) has never been given to us, but it has been put at our disposal — just as a shipping-line puts a ship at a captain's disposal in order that he may work for the company in the shipping business; the ship is not a gift. When God lets us remain as part of His creation and when nature continues to co-exist with us, then the man who feels rich because of what he once possessed will say: Many permissible things have yet been left to me. The other, who would never deny that he loves his work and enjoys life as a feast, says in his turn: Be on your guard against single-track theology, for the man who realizes he has been appointed by God as a captain of the ship of the eternal Ship-owner has to admit: I have received firm *mandates*: there is still work to be done. As for nature — of which I am part, together with my cultural urge — many things must still happen to it before the world will perish; or, rather, will be transferred (into a different mode of existence). The mandate to develop it in and outside myself as God's office-bearer has never been withdrawn — which is a serious warning against Pallieter-axiology.

Culture is a question of *must*. It, too, fell under the original "command of life," of life in its broadest sense. This expression does not mean that there is a command: Live! Nor is it: Man, dare to live! But it means that there is a command that does itself impart life to everyone who obeys it.

Therefore the contents of our cultural calling are never determined by our aptitudes or tastes, as if these could determine the norms, for the primary calling is for everyone: to be sound and whole, *teleios* in the sense of Christ's saying to us: be ye therefore perfect, fully grown, human but never humanistic. Everyone, together with all that belongs to him and with what belongs to the community, has to present himself before God. Not everyone has the aptitudes required for participation in every cultural phenomenon. Variety of natural abilities is not culpable. However, not to posses the ability to engage *directly* in one cultural field or another (e.g., music) is not the same as wilfully to exclude oneself from it. To look upon the cultural struggle as a whole without showing any interest is the opposite of striving for service-conscious training.

Therefore we cannot agree with those who, with Abraham Kuyper, state that Christianity or Calvinism cannot and should not design its own artistic style. Someone has said that Calvinism has failed to develop its own artistic style because its concern is religion and it was forced to leave the "lower" things in favour of the "higher" ones, or at least was not able to develop the former. In our opinion the danger of once again separating religion and culture is imminent here. Besides, the impression is then created that it would be possible to design a style for the one "area of life" and not for the other. "Style" is always first a matter of the whole building, and only then of its respective parts. If a Calvinist can speak of a life-style, he can also speak of an artistic style. We are afraid that the founder of the Free University has limited its task too much. The service of God is above all creative, shaping, and also stylizing. In so far as Calvinism — to mention no more — did *not* develop its own style in any field, this shortcoming is *partly* (for the above-made reservation is still in force) a sign of weakness. If culture is a matter of the everyday service of God, this calling is and remains inexorable, within the limits of each period of the history of salvation as these limits are set by Christ's governing, and everyone has to strive to be a whole and complete man, proportionally and in cooperative relationships set up according to norms that correspond with their purposes. For this calling is never without social effect.

27. Because the balloting norms of these cooperative communities are their peculiar norms, derived from the Law, the preaching and administration of which has been entrusted to the communion of saints, therefore the *fifth* consequence of our standpoint has to be the deep reverence which, also from the cultural viewpoint, may be demanded for the Church.

As the King of the Church, Christ is the King of the whole world also, the One Who completes nature in its history (for Rickert[16] rightly reminds us of the fact that nature, too, has a history), God's Ambassador, who wants to lay down at God's feet all the results of the cosmic process of development and recruitment, and consequently He is also the Governor of culture, and the Judge and Redeemer of its organs. In Him God will "recapitulate" all things (Ephesians 1:10).

We just mentioned Ephesians 1:10 and spoke of a "universal recapitulation." In order to be able to answer the question what particular place Christ has been given with respect to the also culturally to be determined "summary of history," Paul's statement briefly deserves our attention. It says: " . . . that in the dispensation of the fulness of times He might gather together in one all things in Christ." We have derived the phrase "universal recapitulation" from, among others, a translation of Paul's statement as it was quoted by Irenaeus, one of the "Church fathers" (this questionable term is still used to designate children-of-the-Church of a not always harmless kind). Irenaeus (c. 140-c. 202 A.D.) once discussed Christ's ascension into heaven and His sitting at God's right hand with reference to Ephesians 1:10. Where Paul says that Christ will return in order to "gather together in one" all things, Irenaeus' Greek text uses the word *anakephalaiōsasthai*, which in the excellent Latin text of Rouet de Journel is rendered as the Latin verb "to recapitulate."

Ascension Day, seen in this light, means the beginning of this universal recapitualtion.

Does this word help us at all? That depends on the question whether in the rendering of Paul's own word in Ephesians 1:10 it accurately conveys the kernel of the matter. The Vulgate (the official Bible version of the Church of Rome) makes use of a different term in Ephesians 1:10 (instauration) — all the more a reason why the word "recapitulation" calls for our attention.

Many[17] have made use of it. We shall give here just a few examples, which at the same time show us what Paul intended to say.

John Owen (*Works*, I, 147) refers to Ephesians 1:10 when he expresses the opinion that the angels are included in the "recovery" and *recapitulation* of all things which God has given in Christ. Subsequently, he devotes a lengthy treatise to this subject, entitled *The Glory of Christ in the Recapitulation of All Things in Him (pp. 357f)*. Referring to Colossians 1:20, I Corinthians 11:3, Ephesians 1:22 and 23, he extols the power of the redemption whereby that which in God's world had been scattered and broken asunder is re-collected under one Head as one family-of-God, as one body.

Are these interpretations correct?

The Greek word used in Ephesians 1:10 does indeed allow other translations; e.g., "gather together" (KJV), "to unite" (RSV).

It is all a matter of the "atmosphere" from which one thinks this particular word derives, or of the "sphere" to which it points in its imagery.

According to one opinion, this word had its origin in a military setting. When there are soldiers who have lost contact with their troops and are wandering about here and there, one has to try, if possible, to bring them back to their own detachment. This, then, is taken to be the meaning of the word concerned.[18]

However, others offer a different interpretation. They have in mind not so much military operations as arithmetical ones. Adding certain numbers, one gets the "sum," the "result." "Sum" is in Latin *summa*. The idea is that of con-summation. The final sum is made up and underlined, and everyone knows now the result.[19] Christ could

75

then be considered as the one who makes up the final sum, the sum total, showing us: here is everything together. Others have had in mind bookkeepers, who add up amounts of money[20] and give us the result in the final amount.[21]

In the Greek language such a sum-mary, such a summing-up, may be called *kephalaion* (something like: head, principal), and the verb that is used by the apostle Paul is derived from it. According to this train of thought, Christ Himself is the Head, the principal, the sum total. But at the same time (!) "all things" are gathered together, summed up, in this sum (the sum is then included "in" the sum; all things are the sum, including Christ, according to this peculiar train of thought which operates in a somewhat strange way with the words "in Christ").

However, the number of proposed interpretations has still not been exhausted. Others refer to a certain word that was used among the Jews in the days of the apostle Paul. It means so much as "agreement" or "harmony" and is derived from a root that can be translated as "head," or "result of the sum." This technical term would then be in harmony with the Greek word *kephalaion*, and consequently its meaning would be "being brought together (added up)," as well as "being in harmony with each other"; *ergo*: "being gathered together in peace."[22]

We should like to mention a last opinion, one that points back to the schools of the rhetoricians. There an act such as meant by Paul was a brief summary, in a few main points, of what was earlier explained in a more elaborate way.[23] Usually such a summary was not a "neutral," dispassionate summing up, but it was accompanied by a sort of "application": an admonition, a castigation, a word of consolation, or a conclusion stating a demand, as in a court case.[24]

One also encounters various combinations of these etymologies and interpretations. For instance, someone has the boldness to teach that man is a microcosm, a world-in-miniature, comprising the elements of the created world as in a summary; that Christ, as the second Adam, is God and man in one Person; and that man (that compendium of "all things," that microcosm) will finally be re-united with the eternal Word, the Logos.[25] Or: just as sometimes in civil affairs a "member" that has been separated from its "head" (e.g., a woman separated from her husband, the head) is brought back to her "head" and so returns "home," the community to which it belongs (e.g., a woman is brought back to her family), so the whole creation, now separated from God, will return to Christ its Head, and be "home" again.[26] The creation is in that case the reconciled party.[27]

As one can see, the opinions vary greatly.

Whoever wants to come to his own decision has to consider that the Greek word used here does not go back to *kephalē* (head), but to *kephalaion*. The latter has clearly the meaning of "summary," as e.g. in Romans 13:9 and Hebrews 8:1. In Romans 13:9 Paul says that the commandments of the second table can be summarized in the sentence, "Thou shalt love thy neighbour as thyself." This is in all these commandments the ever-recurring main point. It is the summary of the Law. In Hebrews 8:1 the author states: "Now of the things which we have spoken this is the sum: We have such an high priest" as has been introduced to us in the New Testament. This is the sum of the whole argument. But whoever announces a sum or summary, closes his books at the same time. This is how God in the fullness of time will give the sum of history, of the history of "*all things*." He will give the *sum*, not its summary in a sort of "microcosm," a "compendium" of all cosmic elements, an "extract" of all that lives and moves. No, He will give the sum *of* and *in* the history of all things. He will give them for Himself (medium). He will for Himself bring all things to and in their sum,[28] as one could translate freely.

Is this not a *universal recapitulation*, the completing and drawing up of the sum of history? It is *universal*: for "all things" will be involved in it and brought to their con-sum-mation.

However, these "all things" were no stationary quantities; they were permanently in motion. In them the one history was enacted. The sense thereof we understand not from those things nor from their movement itself. For, as we said elsewhere also, the enigmatic aspect does not lie in the spoken or written Word of God, but in the facts, in history itself. We understand the things and their movements only in and from God's Word.

As a matter of fact, no one among men is able, in the manner of a rhetor, to comprise the sum of the history of all things in any formula, not even if he were to stand on his rhetor's toes. For we see only piece-work, and we ourselves are only piece-work. Even the Messiah confesses His inability in this respect: "But of that day and hour knoweth no man . . . but My Father only" (Matthew 24:36).

But *God* is the great Rhetor-Speaker, and also the great Poet-Creator. So *He* is revealed as the *only* Recapitulator-Counter. His counting or adding is not the act of a child that does its sums, but that of the *administrator of time*: He is really *doing* something. He forces things to the end, to the decision. He speaks in Word and fact. In His Word He gives us revelation; in the facts He Himself is revealed. It is for that reason that *He* can make our sums and indeed does make them; our sums are His sums. He had them already in mind even before our life began. He is like the orator who grips his audience and keeps their attention: *what will he say next?* But then suddenly he says: "Thank you," or "Amen." The speaker himself knows full well when he has come to his conclusion, his epilogue, in which he summarizes all that he has said and so brings his oration to a close, to the sum-in-words. But because we have to do here with God, Who is not only the Speaker but also the Maker, the epilogue to His speaking is at the same time the end of His acting. Because His doing is also speaking and His speaking also doing, therefore, as soon as He has arrived at the sum-of-revelation, He at the same time has arrived at the sum-of-action. He completes His historical speaking, and also His historical acting and labouring and moving of all things. "The prayers of David the son of Jesse are ended," it says in the book of Psalms (Psalm 72:20). The Greek translation has: they are brought to *anakephalaiōse* — the same word as in our text. The reflexive summary given by the rhetor and the closing act of the worker are the same — *but with Him only.*

And all this is done by God "in Christ." Not only in Him as the Son (Logos) Who from eternity is closely related with the Father and the Spirit as their Equal (as in Colossians 1), but also in Him as the *glorified Saviour,* Who is seated and has been placed at the right hand of God. In this glorified Christ, God reigns over all things, for good and evil, in blessing and judgment. In Him He brings all things to their end, their consummation, as He has thought it out in His counsel and as He in His speaking and acting has revealed and realized it.

For this is the great significance of Christ's glorification: the Son of man as God's fully authorized Agent has taken all things in hand. God's Oration has passed its half-way mark. History has been brought to a decision. In the great drama the third — and decisive — act has been completed. And now all things must come to their denouement.

The latter, as Paul says, is dominated by Him. There is one single history only, and this is of a "Christian" character, that is, dominated by Jesus Christ. History is also Pneumatic, that is, dominated by the Spirit Who takes it all from Christ. We read our newspaper and listen to the radio, and we grope for the background of what the democrats-in-name in this era of quasi-democracy systematically withhold from us in their deceptive press and their secret diplomacy. We cannot find the sum. No rhetor says exactly what he means. He himself does not even know his own sums, for the historical developments carry him along and the programmes are things belonging to certain periods, and these periods are becoming shorter and shorter. But our God in Christ has the sum in His mind, and when He presently will end all that happens, then we at once will see the sum of His policy. And blessed is he who then will not be overcome by it.

For the sum of "all things" is dominated by Christ, but He has been given as "Head" to the "congregation," and to her alone. He has been put, not in the centre of all things, as their compendium or microcosm, but has been set above and over all things, as their absolute Regent.

*In the Head of the Church the sum of all things is drawn up.* This statement destroys the theory according to which the Church itself is a cultural state or is allowed to become one. No encouragement is here given to any suggestion that the Church — which always, as institute, is to be instituted and therefore never gives away the name of Church to whatever else, in order to characterize the Christian communion in school, family, social life, political life, etc., is falsely called *"the Church as organism"* — is *directly* a practical cultural business, let alone an exponent of culture. This sort of concept concerning the Church would murder her, violate her. In a service in which the Word is preached, the Church does not present a direct lecture on culture that goes into all sorts of technical details, a thinly disguised university for the people. But, on the other hand, the administration of God's Word does put the whole of life under promises and norms. And God has closely connected great promises with the official ministry of the Word, which is the administration of "the seed of regeneration" (Romans 10:17). Faith regenerates, says Article 24 of the Belgic Confession. And this regeneration then takes place in the Church, which brings forth children through the Word of God. It is in this way that the Church can, must, and is allowed to be a hearth where the man of God is from on high "charged" with strength from on high. *From the Church,* where the Spirit of Christ distributes the treasures of grace obtained by Him, the people of God have to pour out over the earth in all directions and unto all human activities, in order to proclaim over all this, and also to show in their own actions, the dominion of God, the Kingdom of heaven. From the Church the fire of obedience, the pure cultural glow included, must blaze forth all over the world. Take the Church away and the Kingdom of God becomes a nebulous affair. Put the Kingdom of God in the mist and the Christ is renounced, also in matters of culture. It is in the *Church* that Christ lets the Spirit procreate children of God. Only the *Church,* as the mother of believers, brings forth the "new" men, who, also as far as cultural life is concerned, bear the burdens of the whole world. Only the *Church* joins them together into an unbreakable communion and teaches the norms for all the relationships of life, even outside the Church. The Church alone (not a so-called clergy!) is the bearer of God's Word, and can in a national community proclaim the norms of God in the language of the time and place concerned and so make known to that community what riches can, according to its own nature, be developed in its life, and how this can and should be done. In the days when the Christian Church was strong, Christian art flourished, and culture was a matter of turning the people's faces heavenward. Today we have sunk to the low level of screaming films and of a theatre that can maintain itself only if inferior items are not dropped from its programmes, of newspapers that depend on a lay-out of sensational headlines, of radio-plays in which a novel is compressed into dialogue form with claptrap as *method*, even of a Church-porch that lacks the courage to keep the announcements of all those busy acctivities from its notice-board. And a community of men that no longer reads articles but only devours their headlines, presently allows *itself* to be devoured. It is an easy prey for the day-texts and ephemeral slogans that make the universal and impertinent corruption by wilfulness and self-worship in business and trade, in press and politics, into one wholesale outpouring of sin, which has been organized so well and so rapidly that it hits the individual with a feeling of impotence that is no longer even given the time to shudder at itself.

Therefore, for the benefit of a Christian culture, that is, a culture that is faithful to its own sense and purpose, all must work with might and main for the upbuilding of the *Church*, of the body of Christ. Take the Church away and what is really human is gone, while humanism, boasting about its own ruins, returns. Take the Church and its confession away and the cultural *hubris* (though in the shape of humbleness) will return which in the heyday of philosophical Romanticism mesmerized the whole German nation, and others, by its immanentistic pantheistic creed of an autonomous and autarkic oscillation of all individually *Gebildete*[29] along with the divine spirit that blows throughout the whole universe. For it is true that in its last period the Romantic school of the day, by the mouth of the Schlegel brothers, simultaneously contradicted just about all its own slogans as derived from Fichte, but its deepest root, the doctrine of man as growing up together with God, has not been rooted out: National Socialism with its cultural projects is proof of that. Take away the Church — which, starting from the local fellowship of the believers, will presently establish national and even international connections — and what is then left will be only an oscillation of "cultural struggles" that put the *strongest* on the throne. The pantheistic slogan concerning "the" right that is inherent *in* things may establish tribunals which sentence people not in the name of the divine Legislator Who by the grace of God made kings cultural shepherds, but in the name of "justice" (Seyss Inquart).[30] Then "the right of the strongest" is the most simple judicial formula. Formulas of justice and of power merge at last. And so, by deterioration in the Church and over the dead bodies of the Church members, a platform is built for the dictator of the last days, Antichrist. He will drill them all according to his system, which is the most horrible of systems. The Church should not be even the smallest direct centre of culture, but she *must* be the greatest indirect cultural *force*. She is the Bride of Christ, that is, the Bride of such a Bridegroom Who, unto Himself and unto His God, brings together all the glory of the nations, and Who is building a city of the finest symmetry. Hence the cubical form of the New Jerusalem.

**28.** The *sixth* consequence is that only through following Christ the individual can become of value for cultural life. Culture is always a communal act. But every communion that has not been bound together by God's Spirit lets the multitude vegetate on the individual and usurp his rightful position. Sometimes — a dictator hailed as a saviour is proof thereof — it leaves itself (and the individual leaves this communion) under the impression that this service of the individual to the multitude is his divine and unfading ornament, and consequently they make him the object of their adoration and worship. A national movement that is based on such a foundation may stir and carry along the masses but it kills the individual personality. What is introduced as *involvement* is nothing but *conformity*. But when in the Old Testament the Law of Sinai addresses itself, not to the Church in general but to the individual Israelite, and when in the New Testament the Sermon on the Mount, that great Canon also of culture, does the same thing, then even in cultural life the individual is in any communal struggle always the one directly concerned, the one addressed by God. Only he who has wittingly and willingly become an office-bearer in following Christ and through Christ, preserves, in the suction of often whirling cultural currents, his personal *idion* in the midst of the ondriving force of the massive formations of "manpower" that drag along the individual or tread him under foot. "Manpower" — it is the querulous term usually reserved for the description of an army that has been mobilized: kings and dictators are said to make use of such "manpower." As if the boards of "trade unions" do not act in the same way.

But one that has been hewn out of the Rock which is Christ,

will — as far as it is up to him — never separate but always distinguish himself (I Corinthians 2). Just as the Decalogue addressed the individual Israelite, the Sermon on the Mount addresses the Christian individually, as well as others, and the Spirit, joining Himself with the whole of God's Word as it issues forth, by acts of re-creation, establishes a *politeuma* (Phillippians 3:20), of which we are the citizens and which has its centre and royal residence in the heavens, and so on earth works mighty things, in particular in creating a communion. The *politeuma*, or state, which is in heaven will on its part never revolt against a *politeuma* here below. But as soon as the earthly *politeuma* on its part commands the citizens of the heavenly one to deny the latter (and the arena of the struggle that then follows is always a cultural-religious one), yes indeed, then there is that painful inability to stem the tide. But even then, in every period of cultural decadence, the great Steward and Custodian of God preserves "the salt of the earth," so that it is sound and wholesome.

Whoever has been subjected to the Sermon on the Mount will perhaps be astonished when confronted with that strange biblical word that says to him: Do this and that, for otherwise "must ye needs go out of the world" (I Corinthians 5:10). This seemingly accommodating word may make him wonder because, after having heard the Sermon on the Mount, he actually thought he could never again remain quiet and composed when listening to moralizing sermons of accommodation. Is it not a matter of chafing and pinching on all sides? To give and take — does such a system not stand accursed in the Sermon on the Mount? Is not the apocalyptic call, "Come out of her, my people, that ye be not partakers of her sins" (Revelation 18:4), a much more direct and much clearer motif?

The answer is: Not at all. To come out of Babylon is not the same thing as to go out of the world. In biblical language "the world" is often, but not always, identical with "Babylon." To leave the "harlot" (see above) and to pluck her does not mean to condemn womanhood, to renounce nature (Ezekiel 16). Not to be partakers of her sins does not mean: along with her creaturehood to deny or abdicate the *sunousia*. Paul's word in I Corinthians 5:10 therefore does not contradict the style and the complex of thought found in the Sermon on the Mount, but has been organically included therein. For the Sermon on the Mount was addressed to the Christians, also in their capacity as missionaries of God in *this* world and as builders of the *new* world. For this reason a Christian is never allowed to go out of this world. In this distorted world he simply has to fulfil his duty before God. The tension that arises from our continuous conflict with "this" world and the command never to go out of "the" world is ultimately the tension between our lot of being in contact with men (*sunousia*) and our daily duty to fellowship (*koinōnia*). The latter, just as God wants it, belongs in this sinful world to the antilegomena, the things and signs that will always be spoken against.

Take away from the Sermon on the Mount the element of the instruction of office-bearers, and that word about not going out of the world will be misused in a horrible way by "the flesh" as if it were a general pardon and a *carte blanche* to do all that pleases "the flesh." But it is quite the opposite. Someone has said (Prof. B. Holwerda, *De reformatie van onzen "omgang,"* [Utrecht, 1947], p. 15):

> If you wish to use this word, you should take it exactly as it is written there.
>
> It does not mean: when you are in contact with the world you can palter with your principles and not be so punctilious. For Paul said just before: you have been redeemed by the cross of Christ and now you must celebrate the feast of nothing but purity and truth . . . . Everything here stands in the climate of absolute seriousness: it has to do with the cross of Calvary, and therefore you cannot take things easy as far as the Church is concerned, in particular with respect to Church discipline. Do you think that Paul would add now: however, in the world it does not matter so much? On the contrary, he stays in the high climate of perfect seriousness. Because of the cross of Calvary the matter of your social intercourse with the world should be taken with perfect seriousness . . . . Is social intercourse with godless people in the Church allowed? No, it is not, for God gave you the keys of the Kingdom of heaven . . . . Is social intercourse with godless people in the world permitted? Yes, it is, for if you were to refuse it, you would go out of the "world."

**29.** Our *seventh* and final conclusion, then, is that, proceeding from this concept of calling, the concept of office, our Christian cultural philosophy will have to begin reasoning more consistently.

As Christian cultural theoretician one should no longer take "common grace" in the above-rejected sense as startingpoint. The startingpoint must be: the original calling, the task given at creation, the original office — lest we be drugged by cultural optimism or cultural contempt.

As soon as this idea is dropped, even the best among us begin to make mistakes.

Dr. Abraham Kuyper, e.g., in his *De Gemeene Gratie in Wetenschap en Kunst* (1904), p. 44, concedes to Von Hartmann that "religion" in its highest form *divests itself of its artistic garment*. We are afraid that this reasoning about "religion" is pantheistic rather than theistic. We are further of the opinion that "religion" does not dress "itself" but that it makes its prophets liturgists (and not only them) and dresses them all in the robes of office. Even the artist may participate in weaving these garments. No, not the artist exclusively, but the artist, too — no more than anyone else has exclusive use of the loom. "Religion" has never been dressed in artistic apparel, but has provided many an artistic garment with the signature of the office and distributed them as robes of office, on the understanding that this signature would be left on and be tolerated by its bearer. A garment of office should never be put off; rather, its distinctiveness should be renewed time and again. This is why we said that in Calvinism the service of God should come to its own peculiar style in all areas of life, to the extent that the above-discussed "restraint" and "abstinence" do not stand in the way.

Neither do we, with regard to the above-mentioned problem, seek our standpoint in an "inborn religious consciousness," which would then try to express and realize itself in religious culture. For man, also pious man, should not live his life to the full, but he should fulfil his *office*.

One's awareness of his office will always urge him to turn to the revelation of God's Word, in order to learn again what the norms are. "Nature," enigmatically, does not teach us anything unless it is put in the light of Scripture. His permanent awareness of his office, also with regard to his cultural task, makes the Christian as *prophet* reach always for God's Word. It teaches him as *priest* never to confuse the office-tempered love of life and joy in culture as *agape* with the purely natural function of his *eros*, as if by means of the latter God's calling were complied with — Pallieter is a pagan! And as *king* it never lets him reach out for life-for-the-sake-of-life but for his Creator, Whose servant and representative he is.

Thus the core of this problem lies in the second answer of Lord's Day 12 of the Heidelberg Catechism. There John Calvin, through his disciples Ursinus and Olevianus, becomes, by the grace of God, a cultural prophet. He preached and gave depth to the concept of man's office and taught us to understand again how the struggle of sin and grace, of obedience and disobedience, is of paramount importance in culture. Those who have passed through

John Calvin's school will never utter exclamations like those of the people who — with a shudder which, incidentally, we can understand — see how, e.g., technical science is developing in gigantic proportions and then with full emphasis cry out that in technology man has triumphed but he has triumphed to *death: Er hat gesiegt aber er hat sich tot gesiegt* (H. Lilje). This cannot be correct. When someone meets his death in any cultural field, it is never the consequence of any cultural act but only of his own disobedience and unfaithfulness in fulfilling his office. "Every creature of God is good, and nothing to be refused, if it be received with thanksgiving" (I Timothy 4:4). John Calvin's concept of autarky is anti-gnostic.

*JESUS CHRIST AND CULTURE*, now for the last time.

Now the hearts may be opened, and the mouths; now the hands may set themselves to work, and the feet bestir themselves unto service. The man who follows Jesus Christ is splendid and sound in so far as he does so. Apart from that, he professes precisely on his day of assembly and festivity (at the table of the Lord's Supper) that he lies in the midst of death. *Homo est, humani nihil a se alienum putat.* He has also become very concrete in all he does and says. Novalis, the poet of Romanticism, once said:

> Wherever darkness intensifies,
> New life springs, fresh blood courses;
> In order to establish eternal peace for us
> He dives into the flood of life;
> With His hands filled He is standing in our midst,
> Lovingly listening to everyone's prayer.

Yes, indeed, He listens to everyone's prayer, but also to everyone's actions, to the purposeful actions of the sober ones, for "they that be drunken are drunken in the night, but let us, who are of the day, be sober," says a voice from the midst of the choir of Bible-authors (I Thessalonians 5:7). Novalis, a Romanticist on principle, and consequently a pantheist and panchristist, sees life rise up again where darkness intensifies; that is, where contrasts can no longer be distinguished, where the unity of opposites is "experienced," and, consequently, where purposeful action, action that is mindful of the fundamental antithesis, is lacking. But our Christ does not know any soldiers but those who belong to the day (which causes things to be distinguished). We do not have a Christ Who merely listens (to prayers of sentiment) but One Who looks on to see how we handle the spade, the hammer, the book, the needle, the brush, and any other instrument, in order *to draw out of the world* — ourselves included — *all that God has put into it.*

"Eschatological sermons, please!" is the cry of many. But let another then cry out that we should sow, and saw, and fly, and telegraph in an eschatological way. Eschatological "theology" is demanded somewhere. But it is better to speak of eschatological culture everywhere.

Therefore, when Novalis says:

Let us in God's garden, full of blessing,
Faithfully tend the buds and flowers,

then we answer that this world is no longer a Garden of God, that is, a "Garden of Eden." The latter will return. But at this moment the world is a workshop, an arena, a building-site. And the place where one meets God, unlike what Novalis apparently had in mind, is not a secluded corner where the romantically disposed soul practises "religion," in a province set apart for the soul. Neither is it a "universe" placed in twilight, not drawing any boundaries between God and nature. For God's forum is today *His* workshop, which is as wide as the world, and it is there that we find *our* workshop, *our* factory, the smoking oven, the study, the studio; in a word, any province, any non-mathematical plane, where "the man of God thoroughly furnished unto all good works" (II Timothy 3:17), "faithfully tends the buds and flowers," wherever there may be any, but also has his rubberboots on, or pulls out weeds, or develops a desert region.

Is it an "endless task?" Yes, indeed. He knows of nothing but such endless tasks, "fool" that he is — "in Christ." It is the others who are foolhardy, in his opinion. And he is right.

Our cultural task in following Jesus Christ is indeed an "endless task." Blessed is my *wise* ward-elder who does his home visiting in the right way. He is a *cultural* force, although he may not be aware of it. Let them mock him: they do not know what they are doing, those cultural gadabouts of the other side!

# NOTES

[1] Anton Mussert was the "leader" of the National-Socialists in The Netherlands before and during the Second World War (Translators' note).

[2] The Department of Culture (*Cultuur-kamer*) was one of the institutions imposed upon the Dutch by the German occupying forces. Registration was compulsory for e.g. artists - although many of them preferred to cease their activities or perform in secret (Translators' note).

[3] In both cases we have to apply quotation marks. For those who together with Him breathed the air of Palestine, were indeed with Him here on earth at the same time, but His position with respect to and in time yet differed from theirs. And although we today do not see Him living among us, we are nevertheless, as far as time is concerned, His contemporaries; for as the living Kurios He intervenes in our temporal existence. He Who as God and man in one person, always in advance, lives for us and sympathizes with us.

[4] "Jesus" is usually called His personal name and "Christ" the name referring to His office. Of course, there are several elements of truth in this distinction. However, in His case the name Joshua (Jesus) is on purpose, expressly, pleromatically, and therefore, for this one case, exclusively interpreted on the basis of the phrase "He shall save His people" (Matthew 1). Consequently Joshua (Jesus) is the first name-of-office; it regards the material of His office and commission. The second one (Christ) regards the legitimacy, the concrete function and analysis of, and His suitability for this commission.

[5] It has no sense here to argue about the question whether at every place in the Bible that has the Greek word for (God's) "fellow-worker" the right exegesis draws the same conclusions as the above-mentioned ones. For not one single "text" but several require our attention here. Besides, the phrase "God's fellow-worker" has been given a certain fixation in systematic theology since the synergistic struggle.

[6] It can also — even better — be expressed in Greek: *stoicheia* (New Testament).

[7] We take over the word "pluriform" although not without inverted commas — for we do not share its philosophical background, which allows the use of this term to be understood in more than one way.

[8] We are here alluding to the well-known Boethian definition of God as the eternal One. According to this, God has a perfect and *tota simul possessio*, i.e., the possession of an interminable life (a life that cannot be limited). This always remains something reserved for God only. *Tota simul* — at the same time in full measure (cf. *perfectum praesens*).

As for man, however, his life is always terminable (limited because he is a creature). Temporally he does not "possess" life in a perfect sense. His possession is not *tota simul*. In eternity (according to the character of the terminable) he possesses life (in his own way) "perfectly" and also (in his own way again) *tota simul*: there is no longer any growth "in" it.

[9] *Pallieter*, by Felix Timmerman, published in Amsterdam, is a novel "in which the main character embodies the pagan glorification of the body and its lusts for life by running out naked in the spring rains and kissing the grounds" (quoted from Henry R. Van Til, *The Calvinistic Concept of Culture*, page 140, note 4).

[10] See further: K. Schilder, *Is de term 'algemeene genade' wetenschappelijk verantwoord?* (Kampen: Ph. Zalsman, 1947).

[11] "Mystical" is an adjective (cf. mystical union). The substantive "mysticism," however, designates something objectionable: the doctrine and methods of an (alleged) immediate knowledge of God — for which the Scriptures allow no room.

[12] Cf. K. Schilder, *Wat is de Hemel?* (Kampen: J.H. Kok, 1935).

[13] The well-known aria from the opera *The Magic Flute, In diesen heiligen Hallen,* could other than in the "lodge," where it actually belongs, also be sung in Church, without offending too many ears. Why? Because the composer's mind, though drunk with Buddhist motifs, was unable to express its own pagan-teutonic cycle of thoughts in adequate style-forms: the style of the Church, this product of many centuries, was still bothering him because he could not let his paganism (Isis and Osiris) speak (cf. the above-mentioned "silence"). In my opinion, we cannot in this reasoning take our starting-point in common grace but in common impotence, which is the result of the tempering that allows no one to transcend creation.

[14] Franciscus Junius, a theologian of the "flowering" of the Reformation, made a similar statement: *de Deo etiam verum dicere periculosum est* (even to speak the truth concerning God is dangerous).

[15] The author here refers to the declarations made by the above-mentioned Synods on, e.g., presumptive regeneration and common grace and their decision that "nothing should be taught which is not in full agreement with" these declarations, which caused a schism in De Gereformeerde Kerken in Nederland (Translators' note).

[16] Heinrich Rickert (1863-1936) belonged to the "Neo-Kantians" of the early twentieth century (Translators' note).

[17] E.g., à Lapide, who refers to Jerome as a supporter of the translation "recapitulation," and also to Irenaeus. *Bibl. Cr.,* i.l., 92, refers to Desiderius Erasmus, and draws the conclusion that the correct translation is: *ad caput revocare;* which is accepted by Vatablus, who, however, adds: *vel, in summam et compendium redigere* (op. cit., 95). Cf. Clarius (op. cit., 98): *recapitulare, h.e. summatim comprehendere et compendiose instaurare;* and also Zegerus (op. cit., 99): *brevi recapitulatione implere et summatim complecti universa mysteria longo tempore praenunciata.* The translation "recapitulation" occurs frequently, but its interpretation nevertheless varies. On Augustine, see Menochius and others.

[18] Hugo Grotius, Hammondus, quoted in J.C. Wolfii, *Curae Phil. et Cr.,* 1734, p. 23; for Grotius, cf. his *Ann. in N.T.,* and *Bibl. Cr.,* VIII, i.l., col. 106, 113/4. Grotius is not definite: *quae significatio huic loco maxime convenit, Bibl. Cr.,* 106.

[19] Dinant, on Ephesians; cf. Wolfii, 23; Cameron, *Bibl. Cr.,* VIII, 101.

[20] Cf. H. Grotii, *An.n.,* i.l. 884, b.

[21] Leidsche Vertaling (Leyden Translation): *in Christus saamvatten.*

[22] Cf. Cameron, in *Bibl. Cr.,* 1.1.101.

[23] Cameron, 1.1., cf. à Lapide, i.v. 475,b.

[24] Aretius, *Comm. in N.T.,* 1612, i.l. 249.

[25] Irenaeus, quoted in à Lapide, i.l. 475/6. Cf. Photius, quoted in Zanchius. *Opera,* t.VI, 19,b.

[26] Aretius, op.cit.

[27] Aretius, op.cit.

[28] Medium; and further: "the causative idea . . . is not due to the voice, but to the verb itself" (-0-00), Robertson, *Grammar, N.T.,* 2nd ed., 809.

[29] *Gebildete* means literally: people who have been "formed," "fashioned." Within the context of Romanticism, however, this term means: people who have risen to a

level at which they are well aware of their own historicity and individuality (Translators' note).

[30] Seyss Inquart was the *Reichscommissar* during the German occupation of The Netherlands in the forties (Translators' note).